W9-AOY-836

DISCARD

Modern Urban Legends

collected and retold by
David **H**olt and **B**ill **M**ooney

illustrated by **K**evin **P**ope

August House Publishers, Inc.
LITTLE ROCK

Published 2004 by August House Publishers, Inc.

P.O. Box 3223, Little Rock, Arkansas 72203

www.augusthouse.com

Printed in the United States of America

10 9 8 7 6 5 4 3 2 1 HB

10 9 8 7 6 5 4 3 2 1 TPB

LIBRARY OF CONGRESS CATALOGING-IN-PUBLICATION DATA

Holt, David.
The exploding toilet : modern urban legends / collected and retold by David Holt and
Bill Mooney ; illustrated by Kevin Pope.
p.   cm.
ISBN 0-87483-754-5 (alk. paper) — ISBN 0-87483-715-4 (pbk. : alk. paper)
I. Mooney, William. II. Pope, Kevin, ill. III. Title.
GR10.H65 2004
398.2'.0973'091732—dc22   2004043752

The paper in this publication meets the minimum requirements of the
American National Standard for Information Sciences—Permanence of
Paper for Printed Library Materials, ANSI Z39.48.

Contents

Introduction

Why do we like urban legends so much?

There are several good reasons. Urban legends tell us a lot about who we are. (It may be more accurate to call urban legends *contemporary legends* since the word "urban" implies a city setting that doesn't always jibe with the story being told.) Another reason is that urban legends usually tell of recent events that could have actually happened.

The title of this book, in fact, comes from a humorous urban legend found in many variations around the world. It sounds unlikely that a toilet would really explode. In 1989, however, propane gas from a railway tanker car was accidentally introduced into the water main of a small town in south-central Arkansas. A worker had improperly attached the gas line, and the propane, carried at high pressure, forced its way into the water line. A casket company employee was injured when the toilet he was sitting on exploded and he was blown through the bathroom door. Another man heard a burbling sound coming from his toilet. As he entered the bathroom to investigate, that toilet exploded. His nylon jacket melted into his pants. When he returned home from the hospital, he declared he was going to build himself an outhouse. "These inside toilets are too dangerous," he said. "Things come and things go, but when a man sees water burning, it might be time to go." (*Arkansas Democrat*, March 9, 1989)

Urban legends are generally chock-full of irony and often contain an element of the supernatural; and, like folktales of old, they reflect our concerns, our fears, our prejudices, our humor, our love of conflict, and our delight in other people's folly and comeuppance.

Urban legends travel from person to person as swiftly as gossip or rumor. Mark Twain once quipped, "A rumor travels twice around the world while the truth is still putting on its shoes." Like gossip and rumor, urban legends contain grains of truth. Gossip and rumor, however, tell of specific people doing specific things at specific locations, while urban legends are generally about Everyman—and the locale is equally nonspecific. Urban legends usually start with something like, "Did you hear about this guy who…"

Man is a storytelling creature. In fact, it has been said that stories are our native language. And our deep love of stories does not dictate that they all be true; indeed, facts should never get in the way of a good story. Shortly after man learned to communicate, he discovered that stories are the best way to pass along information. Information carried within a story is far easier to remember and reaches a deeper level of understanding than just plain facts. That's why so many urban legends are cautionary tales.

While most urban legends are told in conversation as one- or two-line anecdotes, we have taken (just for the fun of storytelling) some basic urban legends and turned them into full-blown stories with identifiable characters, specific settings, and expanded plots. [Some examples are: "Hide and Seek" on page 47 or "The Fickle Finger of Fate" on page 55.] Other urban legends we have left in their original anecdotal form.

Since we completed our first book and CD of urban legends, *Spiders in the Hairdo* (August House Publishers and High Windy Audio, respectively), the Internet has brought about many changes in the general public's awareness of these contemporary tales. When we first started gathering stories for *Spiders in the Hairdo*, we collected most of them face-to-face from individuals. The excellent published collections were also a great help to us. But today, with the speed of the Internet, urban legends fly around the world in a matter of seconds. There are entire websites devoted to them, even sites determining which ones are true and which ones are simply legend.

We're not sure what effect the Internet will ultimately have on the power of urban legends. Since they have always been told person-to-person as true stories happening to friends of friends (ULs are often known as *FOAF* tales, since they invariably happen to a Friend Of A Friend), the speed and impersonal aspect of the Internet may sap some of the legends' vigor. On the other hand, the Internet is very good at passing along hoaxes, which are really first cousins of urban legends. Look at our "Hot Off the Internet" section for some of the more imaginative hoaxes that are being perpetrated every day.

Many of the stories spawned by the 9/11 disaster are plausible and powerful—e.g., the story of the man who rode the collapsing floors of the World Trade Center all the way to the bottom and walked away without a scratch, or the reports of many phone calls coming from the wreckage, or the ruefully humorous story, "Oops," on page 26.

So, perhaps we should not announce the demise of the urban legend; instead, we herald a new era of modern folktales. We see no let-up in the addition of new twists to older legends, or any drought in the creation of completely new tales. Our unquenchable thirst for stories coupled with all the madness of our modern world ensure that we will continue to generate new urban legends that are guaranteed to titillate, amuse, and terrify. That's what this book is all about.

Idiots on Parade

Fool Me Twice

A customer was signing the receipt for his credit card purchase when the clerk noticed the man had never signed his name on the back of the credit card. She informed him that she could not complete the transaction unless the card was signed. When he asked why, she explained that it was necessary to compare the signature he had just signed on the receipt. So the man signed the credit card in front of her. She then carefully compared the signature to the one he had just signed on the receipt. As luck would have it, they matched.

Aint Misbehavin'

A young medical student was doing his rotation in toxicology at the poison control center when a woman called in very upset because she had found her daughter eating ants. The medical student quickly assured the mother that ants are not harmful and there was no need to bring her daughter to the hospital. The mother calmed down, and at the end of the conversation happened to mention that she had given her daughter some ant poison to eat in order to kill the ants. The medical student then told the mother she should bring her daughter into the emergency room right away. He hung up the phone thinking they should give the mother the same treatment.

Tick-a-Lock

When the young couple arrived at the automobile dealership to pick up their new car, they were told the keys had been locked in it. They went to the service department and found a mechanic working feverishly to unlock the driver's side door. As they watched from the passenger side, the wife instinctively tried the door handle and discovered that it was unlocked.

"Hey," she announced to the mechanic. "It's open!"

To which he replied, "Yeah, I know. I already got that side."

Dead Letter Office

A terrorist who had lost a spoon full of brains didn't put enough postage on a letter bomb. It came back stamped: RETURN TO SENDER. The terrorist couldn't recall what was in it, opened it, and was blown to smithereens.

Deer Crossing

A woman who had recently moved from Brooklyn to a semi-rural area in northwestern New Jersey called the local township administrative office to request the removal of the "Deer Crossing" sign on her road.

Her reason: too many deer were being hit by cars and she didn't want them to cross there anymore.

Do You Know Me?

Harry passed through a speed trap that automatically photographed his car and indicated that he had been exceeding the speed limit by twenty-two miles per hour. He didn't know this, however, until a few days later when he opened his mail and found a ticket for $60 and a photo of his car. Instead of writing a check for the fine, he sent the police a photograph of $60.

The next week, Harry got another letter from the police. When he opened it, he found two pictures—photographs of handcuffs and an empty jail cell.

Lettuce, Turnip and Pea

A young woman went to a local Taco Bell and ordered a taco. She asked the person behind the counter for "minimal lettuce." The young man replied that he was sorry, but all they had was iceberg lettuce.

Come Fly With Me

A man was at the airport, checking in at the gate, when an airport employee asked, "Has anyone put anything in your baggage without your knowledge?"

"If it was without my knowledge," he replied, "how would I know?"

The airport employee smiled knowingly and nodded, "That's why we ask."

Oh, I See!

Two intellectually challenged men came to an intersection. When the light changed they heard a loud buzz.

"What's that noise?" asked the passenger.

"Oh, the stoplight buzzes when it's safe to cross the street. It signals blind people when the light is red," said the driver.

The first man stopped, appalled, and said, "What on earth are blind people doing driving?"

Public Service?

Arriving home from two hours of grocery shopping, Alice lugged into the kitchen two plastic bags filled with canned tomatoes only to see her husband, Hank, standing by the stove, shaking frantically. Alice noticed a wire running from his waist toward an electrical outlet. Thinking quickly what she could do to knock him away from the fatal current, she swung both bags as hard as she could, knocking him to the floor, breaking his arm and cracking four ribs. Until that moment, Hank had been listening happily to his Walkman.

Home, Home, I'm Deranged

A few years ago, some employees of the Boeing Corporation decided to steal a life raft from one of the new 747s. That weekend they took the raft out for a big float trip down the river. While they were picnicking and having a high old time, they were surprised to see a Coast Guard helicopter hover over them and armed soldiers motion them to shore. It turns out that the Coast Guard had homed in on the emergency locator that becomes activated when the raft is inflated. Those Boeing employees are no longer employed.

A Constructive Experiment

A psychology student in New York rented out her spare room to a carpenter in order to nag him constantly and study his reactions. After weeks of needling, he snapped and beat her with an ax, leaving her with permanent brain damage.

Ungrateful Pigs!

Two animal rights protesters were protesting the cruelty of sending pigs to a slaughterhouse in Bonn. Suddenly the pigs, all two thousand of them, escaped through a broken fence and stampeded, trampling the two hapless protesters to death.

A Bucket of Bricks

A young man in New Jersey was working his first day of his first job as a mason's assistant. The mason had just finished the brick façade of a new three-story building and had left a pile of unused bricks on the flat roof of the building. The mason told his new assistant to get the bricks down from the roof and bring them over to a new job site on the other side of town.

The young assistant, wanting to make a good impression, had been afraid to show his ignorance by asking how the bricks should be removed from the roof. There were too many bricks to carry them down the ladder. He knew he didn't have the strength for that. If he threw the bricks off the roof they would surely crack. How could he get them down? Then he saw the pulley that had been built to haul the bricks to the roof. *Ah!* he thought. *All I have to do is reverse the process and lower the bricks to the ground!*

First, he pulled a large metal bucket up to the roof with a rope he had run through the pulley. He tied the end of the rope to a railing and climbed up the ladder to the rooftop. The assistant filled the bucket full of bricks. Then he climbed back down the ladder to the ground. He knew the bucket of bricks would be heavy, so he wrapped the rope around his left hand a couple of times, and untied the end of the rope with his right hand. Unfortunately, the bricks were much heavier than the new assistant had imagined and, the laws of physics being what they are, he immediately shot upwards at supersonic speed.

As the new assistant was being propelled to the roof, he looked up to see—coming toward him—the bucket full of bricks, which was dropping at an equal supersonic rate. When the bucket hit him, it broke his nose and collarbone. The bucket whizzed past him as he continued to speed upwards. The assistant hit the pulley just a moment before the bucket hit the ground. Three of his fingers were broken as they were jammed into the pulley. When the bucket hit the ground, its bottom burst and all the bricks spilled out on the grass. Now the comedy started in reverse. As the unweighted bottomless bucket shot upwards, the assistant started down again. Midway, he felt a terrific jolt in his groin area when one of his legs accidentally slipped through the empty bucket.

The young man gasped and tilted forward, freeing himself of the bucket, and continued his Law of Gravity Demonstration. The force of landing on top of the brick pile broke both of his legs, collapsing him in pain. Even so, glad to still be alive, he let go of the rope and yelled for help.

That was when the bucket hurtled back down, hitting him in the head and fracturing his skull.

Granny Get Your Gun

Following the tragic events of September 11, Mildred Coston, a seventy-two-year-old woman who lived in a Dallas suburb, decided to buy a pistol to protect herself from terrorists. She took the gun to the local shooting range and was instructed on how to use it. She kept it with her at all times.

In mid-October, she drove to a nearby mall to do some Halloween shopping for her grandchildren. When she walked back out to the parking lot, loaded down with purchases, she saw six dark-skinned men sitting in her car. She immediately dropped the packages, pulled the gun from her purse, and began yelling.

"Get out! Get out! I know how to use this thing. You try any funny business and I *will* use it! You're not taking my car to blow something up!"

The men fell out of the car and ran as fast as they could, ducking and weaving, to get away from her.

Mildred felt good about what she had done. She only regretted they got away before she could make a citizen's arrest. Putting her purchases in the back seat, she got in behind the steering wheel, and tried to insert her key in the ignition. It wouldn't fit. Suddenly it dawned on her: *Uh-oh, Mildred, you're in the wrong car.*

She looked around to see if anyone was watching. Satisfied that the coast was clear, she gathered up her packages and scurried to her car parked five spaces away. As she began to drive away, she noticed several security guards moving through the parked cars. Mildred rolled down the window and called out to the closest one.

"Excuse me, but I need to tell you gentlemen about a little *faux pas* I just committed."

"Sorry, lady, I don't have time to talk right now," said one of the guards. "Back in the office, I've got six terrified visitors to this country claiming there's some crazy old woman with a gun out here in the parking lot hijacking cars."

Mildred never went back to that mall again.

Second Coming

ARKANSAS CITY—A Little Rock woman was killed yesterday after leaping through her moving car's sunroof during an incident best described as "a mistaken Rapture" by dozens of eyewitnesses. Thirteen other people were injured after a twenty-car pileup resulted from people trying to avoid hitting the woman, who was apparently convinced that the Rapture was occurring when she saw twelve people floating up into the air and then passed a man on the side of the road whom she claimed was Jesus.

"She started screaming, 'He's back! He's back!' and climbed right out of the sunroof and jumped off the roof of the car," said Everet Williams, husband of 28-year-old Georgann Williams, who was pronounced dead at the scene.

"I was slowing down but she wouldn't wait till I stopped," Williams said. "She thought the Rapture was happening and was convinced that Jesus was gonna lift her up into the sky."

"This is the strangest thing I've seen since I've been on the force," said Paul Madison, first officer on the scene.

Madison questioned the man who looked like Jesus and discovered that he was on his way to a toga party when the tarp covering the bed of his pickup truck came loose and released twelve helium-filled inflatable dolls, which floated up into the air.

Ernie Jenkins, 32, of Fort Smith, who's been told by several of his friends that he looks like Jesus, pulled over and lifted his arms into the air in frustration, and said "Come back here," just as the Williamses' car passed him. Mrs. Williams was sure Jesus was lifting people up into the sky as they passed by him, according to her husband, who said his wife loved Jesus more than anything else.

When asked for comments about the twelve inflatable dolls, Jenkins replied, "This is all just too weird for me. I never expected anything like this to happen."

Rue the Roo

Bernie loved kangaroos. It probably started when his mother read him A.A. Milne's *Winnie-the-Pooh*. His favorite characters were not Pooh or Piglet, but Kanga and Baby Roo. From that time on, Bernie had been absolutely nutty about kangaroos. He had kangaroo wallpaper in his bedroom. He had a kangaroo quilt on his bed, covered with fifteen stuffed kangaroos. Stuffed kangaroos were OK, but he wanted to see a real one.

He badgered his parents until they finally gave in and took him to the zoo in the state capital 250 miles away. Bernie loved watching the kangaroos. He refused to look at any other animals, just stayed all day at the kangaroo enclosure. But, as good as it was, he knew somehow it wasn't as good as seeing kangaroos where they were supposed to be—in the wilds of Australia. His parents were sympathetic but refused to take him to Australia just so he could watch a bunch of kangaroos hopping around.

Bernie's fascination with kangaroos continued even after he graduated from college. His apartment was filled with them—stuffed kangaroos, wood kangaroos, glass kangaroos, bombazine kangaroos, metal kangaroos—every kind except the real kind. He spent most of his weekends at the zoo, continuing his marsupial mania.

When he was thirty, Bernie's company sent him on a business trip to Sydney, Australia. Bernie couldn't believe his good luck. He arranged with his boss to take a week of vacation time while he was there so he could travel to the Outback and see kangaroos in the wild.

He rented a car in Sydney and drove through the Australian bush. At dusk, as he was musing on where he might spend the night, a large red kangaroo hopped out into the road right in front of his speeding car. He heard a loud *thwop*. Screaming, "No! No! No!," he slammed on the brakes, tore out of the car, and raced to the kangaroo lying alongside the road, obviously dead. Heartsick, Bernie knelt beside the six-foot-tall animal and stroked its head.

Then he got an idea.

Everyone in the office knew Bernie's obsession with kangaroos. Before he left on the trip, some of his colleagues had kidded him that the kangaroos would be as nutty about him as he was about them. "Yeah, Bernie, they'll even come right up and pose for pictures with you! You'll probably get some shots of them nibbling your ears!"

Grunting and straining, Bernie managed to prop up the kangaroo. Then, to add a little bit of humor, Bernie ran back to the car and got his jacket. He slipped the jacket on the roo. Then he quickly attached his camera to a tripod, focused the lens, and set the automatic timing device. Racing to get into place before the camera snapped the picture, he put his left arm around the kangaroo and with his right he held the roo's head so that the picture would show Bernie getting a kangaroo kiss.

Just as the flash attachment went off, Bernie felt something moving in his arms. The next moment he was thrown to the ground. As he pulled himself up, he saw the kangaroo hopping away—through the Australian Outback twilight, wearing Bernie's jacket that held his wallet, his keys, and his passport.

QT on the TP

Cletus and Quinton, two old farmers who lived in the mountains of North Carolina, had not been to the city for years and wanted to see how things had changed. They had never seen a modern mall and decided to take a gander. The two men were surprised that no store in the mall sold chicken feed or barbed-wire fencing or tractor parts. Instead they only found fancy stores selling body lotions, designer jeans, and wireless phones.

Cletus suddenly felt the call of nature. He went into the men's room while his friend stayed outside. He stayed in the restroom a long time. When Cletus finally came out, he was bent over and walking funny.

"What's the matter, Cletus?" Quinton asked.

"Hurt my back."

"How'd you do it?"

"Well, these modern places have done away with toilet paper."

"Naw! Well, what in the world do they use now?"

"All they've got is a hot air blower hanging on the wall."

She Got Game

Jennifer carried a load of laundry down the stairs to the basement of her home. As she stuffed the load in the washing machine, she realized the housedress she was wearing hadn't been washed in a while. She pulled it off and placed it in the machine. Then she thought, *I might as well wash all my underclothes too*. She slipped out of them and started the wash cycle.

Turning to go back upstairs, Jennifer noticed a large spider web in a corner of the basement. She picked up a broom to brush it away, then realized she ought to protect herself from the possibility of spiders falling on her. Spotting her son's old football helmet, she pulled it over her head and raised her broom.

Just then she heard a cough behind her. She spun around to see the meter reader from the electric company standing there. Embarrassed, he turned to leave. "Lady," he quipped, "I don't know what team you're playing for, but I sure hope your side wins."

Have a Nice Day

A middle-aged man bought a brand new Mercedes convertible SLK. He took off down the road, speeding up to eighty miles an hour and enjoying the wind blowing through what little hair he had left on his head.

This is great, he thought as he stepped on the gas pedal even harder.

He looked in his rearview mirror and saw a Florida Highway Patrol trooper behind him, blue lights flashing and siren screaming.

I can get away from him with no problem, thought the man. He floored it, flying down the road at over a hundred miles an hour. Then it occurred to him: *What am I doing? I'm too old for this kind of thing*. He pulled over to the side of the road to wait for the state trooper to catch up with him.

The Trooper pulled over behind the Mercedes and walked up to the driver's side.

"Sir," he said, looking at his watch, "my shift ends in thirty minutes, and today is Friday the Thirteenth. If you can give me a good reason why you were speeding—that is, one that I've never heard before—I'll let you go."

The man looked up at the trooper and said, "Last week my wife ran off with a state trooper, and I thought you were bringing her back."

The trooper said, "Have a nice day."

Oops!

In New York City, on the morning of September 11, 2001, a married man went to his girlfriend's apartment in Queens instead of to his office at the World Trade Center. When his wife saw the second plane fly into the side of the building, she called him on his cell phone. She expected the worst, but she was surprised to hear him being so offhand. "No," he said, "just another boring day at the office. Nothing exciting ever happens here."

We don't need to elaborate on what happened later.

Bird Brain

Three brothers were sharing the cost of taking care of their elderly mother. All three had done well in the stock market surge, so for her eightieth birthday, each brother hoped to out-do the other two by giving her an expensive gift.

The first brother sent a new entertainment center, with recessed shelves, and a big-screen TV, DVD player, and stereo built in. When he called his mother she said, "I could never figure out how to use this big thing, but it is a nice place to store my potted plants."

The second brother bought her a new solid silver tea service. His mother told him,

"It looks so beautiful, but I am too old to start polishing silver. Life is too short. I packed it away in the closet."

The youngest brother knew his mother loved to study the Bible so he bought her a parrot that could recite the entire book, chapter and verse. It was the most expensive gift of all, since it had taken many years of constant repetition to train the bird.

When he called her and asked how she liked the incredible parrot she said, "Your present was the best of all. It was absolutely delicious…tasted just like chicken."

Take the Cake, and Credit Too

Marge was supposed to bake a cake for the church women's group bake sale, but she forgot to do it until the last minute. She bought a mix for angel food cake, whipped it up, and threw it in the oven. When she took it out, however, the center of the cake had dropped flat. *Oh, dear,* she thought. *No time to bake another one. I'll just have to make do.*

She looked around the house for something that would build up the center of the cake. She found what she needed in the bathroom—a roll of toilet paper. She plopped it in the center and covered it with icing. *Not bad looking,* she thought, *even if I do say so myself.*

Marge rushed the cake to the church, then hurried back and instructed her daughter to be at the sale the minute it opened. She was to buy Marge's cake and bring it back home. But when the daughter arrived at the sale, Marge's cake had already been sold. She was beside herself.

A couple of days later, Marge was invited to play bridge at a friend's home. Two tables had been set up. After the first rubber, a fancy luncheon was served. And, wouldn't you know it, Marge's cake was presented for dessert.

When Marge saw the toilet-paper angel food cake, she started to rush into the kitchen and tell her hostess all about it. But before she could get to her feet, one of the other women said, "Oh, my! What a beautiful cake!"

Marge fell back in her chair when she heard the hostess reply, "Thank you. I made it myself."

The Value of Undies

Be careful what you wear (or don't wear), when working under your vehicle—especially in public.

From the Sydney (Australia) *Morning Herald* comes this story of a couple who drove their car to K-Mart only to have it break down in the parking lot. The man told his wife to carry on with the shopping while he fixed the car there in the lot. The wife returned later to see a small group of people near the car. On closer inspection she saw a pair of male legs protruding from under the chassis. Although the man was in shorts, his lack of underpants turned his private parts into glaringly public ones. Unable to stand the embarrassment, she dutifully stepped forward, quickly put her hand up his shorts and tucked everything back into place.

As she stood back up, she looked across the hood to see her husband standing idly by. The mechanic, however, had to have three stitches in his head.

Falling Flat

Two Stanford University students decided to take the weekend off to go rock climbing in Yosemite even though they had a big philosophy test scheduled for Monday. The weather was perfect, so it was an easy decision to stay another day and blow off the exam. When they got back to school on Tuesday, they told the professor they had had a flat tire and were unable to get back in time. Could they re-schedule the test?

The professor, being very philosophical, said, "Certainly, since it wasn't your fault. Why don't you make up the test Thursday?"

At the appointed time, the professor greeted them and put them in two separate rooms to take the three-page exam.

They were both amazed at how simple the test was. The questions on the first two pages were easily answered, though they were worth a mere twenty percent of the overall grade. They were shocked, however, when they reached the third page and discovered it was worth eighty percent of the score and contained only one question:

Which tire was flat?

Lips, Lips, Lips

For ten years Mrs. Nichols had seen to it that Hargrove High School and its grounds were kept in tip-top shape. She was its firm-but-fair principal who understood the importance of Order and Discipline. O&D, as she termed it, gave the students a solid sense of respect, not only for their school, but for themselves as well. Mrs. Nichols also understood that kids will sometimes be kids and rebel against O&D. Bucking authority was simply a part of the growing-up process. But the petty vandalism that often went along with it would not be tolerated.

Near the end of the school year, a group of senior girls began putting lipstick kisses on the mirrors in the girls' restroom. It seemed harmless enough, except for the fact that every evening the janitor had to work extra hours to clean the lipstick off the mirrors.

Mrs. Nichols had a good idea as to which girls were marking up the mirrors. The group of twelve young women were not really malicious, she knew, just heedless kids out to have a little fun. If she reasoned with them, surely they would understand and stop. No discipline would be needed. But how could she make her point effectively?

One afternoon the principal called the twelve girls from their classes. As she led them into the girls' restroom, they glanced at each other apprehensively.

"I'm sure you've all noticed," Mrs. Nichols said, "how much our restroom mirrors are being kissed lately." The girls giggled nervously. "Now, I'm not accusing any of you of such a silly act. I just want to show each of you how hard our janitor has to work to clean the lipstick prints off the mirrors."

She then nodded to the janitor, who took a nasty-looking toilet brush, dipped it in a toilet, and began cleaning the mirrors.

Slack-jawed, the girls stared in horror.

From that moment on, no lipstick prints were seen on the mirrors again.

Prophet Without Honor

James Ketchum graduated from UCLA with a B.S. in criminology and entered the U.S. Army. He served for twenty years beginning in the early1940s. He was an investigator of Nazi war criminals during the Nuremberg trials and stayed in Germany for many years following the war, organizing civilian police forces. During that time, he wrote numerous books on criminal justice. Ketchum retired from military service in 1962 with the rank of full colonel.

Returning to California, he began teaching criminology at a large university on the West Coast.. His work was well-respected, but after about ten years of service, he was called to see the president of the college. The president informed Ketchum that he could no longer teach with just a bachelor's degree. Times were changing, he said, and school policy required that faculty members hold graduate degrees. Merely having twenty years of distinguished experience was no longer considered sufficient qualification to teach. All new faculty members were now required to hold a doctorate, the president explained, and the school was actually doing him a favor by letting him keep his job by getting 'only' a master's degree.

James Ketchum enrolled in a summer program at an out-of-state college—three months of intensive seminars followed by nine months of home study would get him his master's degee.

On the first day of class, the instructor was taking roll. He stopped when he read Ketchum's name.

"Are you related to the James Ketchum who wrote the textbook we'll be using?" he asked.

"I *am* the James Ketchum who wrote the textbook you're using," came the dry response.

Take What Comes

Richard Flasher, an honor roll high school student, worked hard at odd jobs after school to earn money for college. He applied to Purdue knowing that, even if he got accepted, he would barely be able to make ends meet.

Much to Richard's surprise, Purdue sent a letter of intent offering him a full basketball scholarship for his freshman year. Richard wasn't a basketball player, but for a free year in college he was willing to do anything. He signed the letter and sent it back.

As it turned out, there were two applicants to the freshman class with the same name. The university, when it realized its mistake, tried to invalidate Richard's letter of intent; the mediation board, however, held the letter of intent to be a legally binding contract.

Richard gladly warmed the bench at basketball games, and the rest of the time he worked diligently at his studies. By the end of the first year he had a straight-A average and was given a full academic scholarship for the next three years.

The Exploding Toilet

Jasper was on his patio working on his motorcycle. His wife, Anne, was in the kitchen preparing dinner. Jasper started racing the motorcycle's engine, and somehow the motorcycle slipped into gear. Still holding the handlebars, he was dragged headlong through the glass patio door, and the motorcycle dumped onto the floor inside the house.

Anne, hearing the crash, ran into the dining room and found Jasper lying on the floor, cut and bleeding. The motorcycle lay next to him, and the patio door was shattered. She ran to the phone and called an ambulance. Because they lived on a fairly large hill, Anne went down the several flights of long steps to the street to direct the paramedics to her husband.

After the ambulance arrived and transported Jasper to the hospital, Anne uprighted the motorcycle and pushed it outside. Seeing that gas had spilled on the floor, Anne got some paper towels, blotted up the gasoline, and threw the paper towels in the toilet.

Jasper was treated at the hospital and released with minor injuries. After he arrived home, he looked at the shattered patio door and the damage done to his motorcycle. Feeling despondent, he went into the bathroom, sat on the toilet, and lit a cigarette. He finished the cigarette while still seated, then flipped it between his legs into the bowl. Anne, who was back in the kitchen, heard first a loud explosion and then the screams of her husband. She ran into the bathroom and found Jasper lying on the floor. His trousers had been blown away, and he was suffering burns all over his buttocks, the backs of his legs, and his groin area. Anne ran to the phone and again called for an ambulance. The same ambulance crew was dispatched, and again Anne met them at the front door. The paramedics again loaded Jasper on a stretcher and began carrying him out to the ambulance.

As they were going down the stairs to the front door, one of the paramedics asked Anne how her husband had happened to burn himself. When she told them, the paramedics started laughing so hard that one of them tipped the stretcher and dumped Jasper out. He fell down the rest of the stairs and broke his ankle.

When Nature Calls ... Answer

Bill had been hard at work for two weeks selling encyclopedias in the Nashville neighborhoods. He worked each neighborhood on foot, carrying his wares from door to door. He had not made a single sale. Late Friday morning, Bill felt a call from nature. Since he had been instructed never to use a prospect's facilities, he began to look for a restaurant or business that would have a public restroom. At the far end of the block, Bill spotted a sign for the Morris Funeral Home.

Hastily, he made his way through the front door and into the men's room. As he was leaving, one of the funeral home attendants asked Bill if he needed help finding the deceased. Not wanting to appear to be a freeloader, he said, "Yes, where is the casket?"

He was led into a large ornate room. Against one wall was a very expensive gold, silver, and walnut coffin. The deceased was a distinguished gentleman in a hand-tailored suit. Even though there were no other visitors, Bill pretended to pay his respects.

As he was leaving, Bill glanced at the open guest book and saw there were no other signatures. *What a shame,* he thought. He filled in his name and address and left.

Three months later, Bill received a letter from a lawyer explaining that, according to the dictates of the deceased's will, all those people who attended his funeral or came to pay respects would inherit his entire fortune. Bill was the only visitor. Enclosed was a check for ten million dollars.

It Pays to Be Nice

Herbert was driving along a deserted road at dusk. As he rounded a curve he saw a man looking under the hood of his car. Herbert stopped his car and offered to help. Fortunately, the trouble was just a loose wire. When the wire was reconnected and the car started again, the grateful man asked Herbert for his address to send him a reward for helping him. Herbert declined and said he wanted nothing, but the other man kept insisting so finally he gave in. Then both men got in their cars and drove off.

Two weeks later, Herbert received a letter from his bank stating that his home mortgage was paid in full. He called the bank and said there must be some mistake.

"No," said the loan manager, "Bill Gates was quite insistent that you own your house free and clear."

Just a Green Snake

Green garden grass snakes can be dangerous. Yes, grass snakes, not rattlesnakes.

A couple in Rockwall, Texas, had a lot of potted plants. During a recent cold spell, the wife brought a number of them indoors to protect them from a possible freeze. It turned out that a little green garden grass snake was hidden in one of the plants. When the snake had warmed up, it slithered out, and the wife saw it go under the sofa. When she let out a scream, her husband, who was taking a shower, ran out naked into the living room to see what the problem was.

The wife told him there was a snake under the sofa. Right after he got down on his hands and knees to look for it, the family dog came into the room and cold-nosed him in the behind. Positive that the snake had bitten him, the husband fainted. His wife, however, thought he'd had a heart attack, so she called the emergency squad. The attendants rushed in and loaded him on the stretcher and started carrying him out.

About that time, the snake came out from under the sofa and the Emergency Medical Technician saw it and dropped his end of the stretcher. The fall broke the husband's leg, and he wound up in the emergency room. The wife still had the problem of the snake in the house, so she called her next-door neighbor to come over and help. The neighbor, armed with a rolled-up newspaper, began poking under the couch. He soon decided the snake was gone and told the wife, who sank down on the sofa in relief. As she relaxed, her hand dangled in between the sofa cushions, where she felt the snake wriggling around. As she screamed and fainted, the snake rushed back under the sofa, and the neighbor, seeing her lying there unconscious, tried to bring her to by using mouth-to-mouth resuscitation.

The neighbor's wife, just returning from grocery shopping, saw her husband's note that he was next door. As she walked through the open door, she was shocked to see her husband's mouth on the neighbor woman's mouth. She slammed her husband in the back of the head with a bag of canned goods, knocking him out and cutting his scalp to a point where it needed stitches. The noise woke the woman from her dead faint, and she saw her neighbor lying on the floor with his wife bending over him, so she assumed he had also been bitten by the snake. She went to the kitchen, brought back a small bottle of whiskey, and began pouring it down the man's throat.

By now the police had arrived. When they examined the unconscious man and smelled the whiskey, they assumed a drunken fight had taken place. The police were about to arrest them all, when the two women tried to explain that it all had happened because of a little green snake. The police summoned an ambulance, which took away the neighbor and his sobbing wife. Just then, the little snake crawled out from under the couch. One of the policemen drew his gun and fired at it. He missed the snake but hit the leg of the end table on one side of the sofa. The table fell over, the lamp on it shattered, and the bulb broke, starting a fire in the drapes. The other policeman tried to beat out the flames and fell through the window into the yard on top of the family dog, who, startled, jumped up and raced into the street, where an oncoming car swerved to avoid it and smashed into the parked police car. Meanwhile, the burning drapes spread to the walls, and soon the entire house was blazing.

Vigilant neighbors had called the fire department and the arriving fire-truck started raising its ladder when it was still half a block away. The rising ladder tore out the overhead wires, disconnecting the electricity and telephones in a ten-square city block area.

Time passed, and both men were discharged from the hospital, the house was re-built, the police acquired a new car, and all was right with their world.

About a year later, however, the husband and wife were watching TV. When the weatherman announced an approaching cold snap, the husband asked his wife if she thought they should bring in the plants for the night.

And that's when she shot him.

God Helps Those Who Help Themselves

A small congregation just inside the city limits of Wheeling, West Virginia, built a new church on a parcel of land willed to them by a deceased church member. The congregation had very little money and built the church themselves, much in the fashion of old "barn-raisings." Since they did the work themselves, they didn't take the time to learn all the ins and outs of the local building codes.

Ten days before the new church was to open, a local building inspector arrived and informed them that the parking lot was not large enough for the size of the building. The members of the congregation pleaded with him to be lenient, but the inspector would not budge from his position.

"Because of your own mistakes, you won't be able to use it as built. Until you double the size of your parking lot, you can't use this sanctuary."

The congregation was distraught. They had used every inch of their land except for the steep hill against which it had been built. To achieve more parking spaces, they would literally have to move the hill behind them.

The next Sunday morning when all the worshippers gathered for the service, the pastor surprised them by saying, "I want all of you who believe that faith can move mountains to stay. The rest of you can go home. I want no scoffers or non-believers here."

Of course no one left.

"This morning, instead of the regular service, we're going to hold a prayer meeting and ask God to help us remove this hill from our back yard and somehow furnish us with enough money to have it paved over before our opening dedication a week from today."

All eighty members of the congregation fell to their knees and began to pray in earnest. The children of the church prayed for as long as they could, but the adults stayed on their knees for nearly three hours. Finally, the pastor said, "Amen." Then, as everyone rose stiffly to their feet, he added, "We're going to open our doors next Sunday just as we planned. God has never let us down before, and He won't let us down this time."

Although they had spent three hours at prayer, not all the congregation was as certain as the pastor of God's intentions. In fact, some of them thought their preacher might have tempted Providence by making such a bold prediction.

The next morning, just as the pastor was finishing breakfast, he heard a loud knock at the front door of the manse. Opening the door, he saw a beefy construction worker wearing a hard hat standing on his front stoop.

"Pardon me for not calling first, pastor, but I wanted to catch you as soon as I could," said the man. "I'm the foreman for Tillinger Construction Company here in Wheeling. We're building that big shopping center on the other side of town—you probably read about it in the papers—and we need a humongous amount of fill dirt for the parking lot. I was wondering if you folks would be willing to sell us some of that hill right behind the new church you're building?"

The pastor was so surprised he could not speak.

The construction foreman took his silence as reluctance and went on, "Now, I know we're asking a lot, but we could pay you nicely for the dirt we take away."

The pastor still had not found the words to express his gratitude, so the foreman continued.

"You see, pastor, we're kind of between a rock and a hard place. We can't do any more construction on the shopping center until we get that dirt in there and let it settle. We need to move it in right away. We thought we had enough landfill, but our engineers misjudged it pretty badly, which is why I'm out scouting around for some dirt. What do you say?"

The pastor's eyes teared up, but still his words would not come.

"Tell you what, pastor. That exposed area where we take away the dirt—we won't leave it looking ugly. Why, as soon as we get it out, I'll have my men come over and pave it for you. And, we'll landscape it around the edges. Why, we'll even landscape your whole property if you'll let us have the dirt. I know this is an unusual request, but we need to find some landfill and right away."

The little church held its dedication the very next Sunday, just as planned. Not only were all the members of the church there, but so was the city building inspector as well as the construction foreman and all his crew. And the title of the sermon was "Faith Can Move Mountains."

If It's Not One Thing, It's Another

The average cost of rehabilitating a seal after the Exxon *Valdez* oil spill in Alaska was $80,000. At a special ceremony, two of the most expensively saved animals were released back into the wild amid cheers and applause from onlookers. A minute later, in full view, they were both eaten by a killer whale.

Scary Stories

Hide and Seek

Becky was a wild child who did anything she wanted. She lived with her parents in a beautiful mansion in Palm Beach. They gave her everything she wanted ... except their attention. In trying to get her parents to show some concern, Becky pulled every prank she could think of to get herself noticed. Whenever the principal sent her home from school, she would disappear for days, just to rile her parents. She once brought a bottle of gin to high school and showed it to everybody, which guaranteed her expulsion.

When she reached eighteen, Becky told her parents that she was getting married. She had only known her fiancé three months and he was something of a wild hair himself. Becky told her mother she was tired of going to school and didn't want to go to college. She didn't really love the boy. Since his family had "old money," she joked that this was to be a marriage of convenience. Her parents were shocked but relieved. They saw no better opportunities for Becky, so they agreed to pay for the wedding.

As her father escorted her down the aisle, Becky looked stunning in a beautiful hand-made wedding dress covered with white sequins. The wedding was followed by a fancy reception for four hundred guests at the country club. Afterwards, the young people moved the party to a forty-room estate belonging to the groom's deceased grandparents. The unoccupied old house, full of antiques and overstuffed furniture, was a perfect place for a late night party. Now the celebration could begin in earnest.

About three in the morning, Becky demanded that the guests play hide and seek. After the young husband was declared "it," all the party guests scattered in search of places to hide. That was easy; the old mansion had hundreds of great hiding places. It wasn't until the sun came up that the groom found all the hidden guests.

All, that is, except Becky.

By now, everyone was sober. They spread throughout the huge house looking for her. "Come on," they called out. "The game's over." By noon, their worry gave way to exasperation. They were beginning to suspect that this was just another one of Becky's pranks. Maybe the whole wedding had been a prank.

When Becky's husband told her parents she was missing, they immediately called the police to investigate. The officers conducted a thorough search of the house and grounds but found no trace of her. Once they learned about Becky's rambunctious past, coupled with her parents' admission that she didn't love her new husband, the police surmised that Becky had run away to get out of the marriage before it could start.

The police helped the parents file a missing person's report, but nothing new turned up. After three years, the case was declared inactive. The rejected young husband found a new love, remarried, and started a family. Becky's parents hired a private detective to track down their daughter, but he was never able to find her.

Ten years later, the old estate where the party had been held was put up for sale. A wealthy young couple bought it, antiques and all. One day, as they were exploring some of the back bedroom closets, they discovered a large dusty trunk hidden behind a rack of old clothing. The trunk was locked. When they pried the latch open, there in the bottom lay the curled-up skeleton of a young woman—wearing a beautiful wedding dress covered in white sequins.

Fancy

Henry Meeker owned a cattle ranch outside a small Texas town along the Leon River. He was a shy, quirky little fellow who kept mostly to himself. But every Saturday night he would show up at the Mustang Saloon and quietly drink himself into oblivion.

Henry had never married and knew virtually nothing about women, but that didn't stop him from falling in love with a dancing girl at the Mustang. Miss Francie Parker was tall and curvy with a long mane of red hair. Everyone called her "Fancy" because of the pretty dresses she wore trimmed with colorful ribbons and bows.

What Henry liked most about Fancy was her devilish little smile, which seemed to imply that a cute trick was soon to be played on somebody. All the men liked her for the way she teased and joked with them, but Henry adored her. He thought Fancy was the most beautiful woman he had ever seen. He couldn't take his eyes off her. When she was serving in the saloon, he would order drink after drink just so he could talk with her. His extravagant tips always got her attention—at least while he was in the saloon.

One day, Henry worked up enough courage to ask Fancy to marry him. She laughed and said, "Henry Meeker, I don't need a husband. I need a wife! Someone to do for *me.*"

"Aw, Fancy," said Henry, "come live with me and I'll do everything for you. I'll be your husband, your wife, your servant. I'll cook, clean, make the money. Marry me and you won't have to do anything but sit around all day and wear pretty dresses. I'll do anything for you, Fancy."

Fancy knew he had money because of the large tips he left her. *Maybe marrying Henry wouldn't be so bad*, she thought. *He'd be easy to control. He'd do anything for me—give me a house and money. I'd never have to work. In fact, I wouldn't have to do anything if I didn't want to.*

One day, on a lark, after he had again asked her to marry him, she joked, "Get me that new green taffeta dress with the lace collar in the window of the dress shop and I'll marry you." She knew she was safe since the dress cost as much as most ranchers made in a year.

The next morning, the dress was waiting for her at the saloon—still on the mannequin. The note pinned to it read, THE WEDDING WILL BE THIS SATURDAY. Fancy quit the saloon and married Henry.

At first, things went well. Even though Henry wanted Fancy all to himself and wouldn't let her leave the house, he placated her with gifts—new dresses, nice furniture, china, silverware. It was only a short time, however, before Fancy, who had spent her young life joking and frolicking with men, became restless. One night, she got fed up.

"Henry, I'm going into town," she said. "Don't try to stop me or I'll never come back."

She saddled a horse and rode away. It drove Henry crazy that she could be seeing other men. From that day on they argued constantly, but nothing he said ever stopped her from going into town alone.

He finally realized no matter what he said or did, he couldn't hold her back. *If I can't have her*, he thought, *then nobody can.*

That's when he decided to kill her.

Henry wasn't the kind of man who picked up a gun and shot somebody. He certainly didn't relish the idea of dangling from the end of a rope or spending the rest of his life in jail. So he began to think of ways to kill Fancy that would seem like a natural death.

One day as she was getting ready to go into town, Henry said meekly, "I'll saddle up your horse for you." She was surprised to hear this but figured she had finally broken him from trying to stop her. Out in the stable, he cut the saddle's girth strap almost all the way through, so that any sudden movement would cause the saddle and rider to fall off. Fancy always rode hell-for-leather. Henry felt certain this would get her.

Dressed in her green taffeta dress, Fancy mounted the horse side-saddle. As she rode off toward town, she flashed him a devilish smile. *Yes, I've finally beaten you*, it seemed to say. Henry fretted all day, wondering if his plan had worked. At dusk, she arrived home bedded down in the back of a buckboard driven by Spreader Bass, a tall, handsome, silver-haired man.

Henry ran to the wagon.

"Fancy, what happened to you?"

"Your beautiful wife has had a bad accident," said Spreader Bass.

"The cinch broke just as she was fording the river. Looked to me like it'd been cut. She fell in and hit her head on a rock. Lucky I came along and pulled her out. Took her to Doc Lowrey and he fixed her up. She'll be all right in a few days, but she needs bed rest. You need to take better care of her, Henry Meeker."

Every day after that, Spreader Bass looked in on Fancy. The way she smiled at him in her impish way, Henry knew something was beginning to happen between them. As she got better, Spreader took her out for afternoon rides in his buckboard—each ride getting longer and longer. Whenever they left, Henry tried to stop her from going, and each time she laughed at him.

Henry began to devise a way to kill Fancy—no mistake about it.

One night, Henry cooked her favorite meal—tomatoes and okra, smothered in onions … and laced with nightshade, a deadly plant that grows everywhere in Texas. Henry served her bowl after bowl. After a while Fancy began to feel dizzy, then she became nauseous and clammy. Her hands started to tremble and she broke out in a cold sweat. When her arms began to go numb, she realized what was happening to her. She tried to get up, but she couldn't move her legs.

Fancy looked into Henry's eyes and said, "You're doing this to me, aren't you? You're trying to kill me. First you cut the saddle cinch. Now you're trying to poison me. I warn you, I'll come back. I swear I will. And I'll get you, you little weasel. I'll get you good."

By the end of the day, Fancy was dead.

Henry told the doctor that his wife hadn't been the same ever since her fall from the horse. The doctor ruled that she had died of natural causes. At the funeral, folks said she looked so pretty in her green taffeta wedding dress—even had that devilish little smile on her lips. She was buried in the graveyard on the bluff of the river.

Soon after the funeral, Henry started going back to the Mustang Saloon every Saturday to drink away his guilt. He sat in his same seat at the corner of the bar. It felt good to be back. He hadn't been there since he married Fancy.

One stormy spring day, Henry arrived early at the Mustang. It had rained for two days. The river was rising but Henry didn't seem worried about making it home. He still had a lot of liquor to get past his lips. Through his drunken haze he heard ranchers talking about moving their herds to higher ground and families getting trapped by the floodwaters. The rain kept falling and the water kept rising and Henry kept drinking. The river soon flooded its banks and began to force its way into town. When Henry stumbled to the window to take a look, Main Street looked more like a river than a road. Deciding he'd better start for home, Henry lurched out of the saloon, off the steps, and into water up to his knees—boiling, swirling, dangerous water. All kinds of things were floating in the flood—trees, crates, furniture—things that could kill a man. Telling himself he had to get home, Henry picked up a stick to help brace himself against the floodtide. Some of the people in the saloon yelled for him to come back, but on he went.

He was halfway across the street when he looked up and saw a strange sight—coffins floating down Main Street. Tumbling floodwaters had torn the coffins out of the graveyard and sent them careering into town. He hurried to get across the street, but the coffins were bearing down on him. One of them turned broadside and headed straight for him. He struggled to get out of the way but could barely move in the raging water. The people trapped in the buildings watched in horror as the coffin hit Henry, the pine boards splitting, the lid flipping open.

They couldn't believe their eyes as they saw Fancy's stiffened body burst from the coffin—her green taffeta dress enveloping Henry as he fell into the raging flood. It seemed to those who watched that Fancy had thrown her arms around Henry. Desperately, he thrashed about, struggling, trying to keep his head above the water. Fancy seemed to hold him tightly as they were swept down stream.

The water didn't recede for three days. When it finally did, debris was everywhere. Pieces of furniture, logs, even bodies were lodged thirty feet up in trees. A week later, five miles downstream, Henry and Fancy were found, caught in the branches of an old pecan tree, their arms wrapped around each other. It's said that when they were taken down—even after all that—Fancy still wore her devilish little smile.

Body and Soul

The Greens, a retired couple, were driving down a winding road in the Pocono Mountains of Pennsylvania. As they topped a small hill they could see in the roadway up ahead a red-headed woman signaling for them to stop.

"I wonder what she wants. Looks like she might be in some trouble, Maggie."

"Don't stop, George, it's probably a trick. I've been reading how these people lure you into stopping, pretending there's a wreck or something. Then they knock you in the head and take your money."

"Aw, Maggie, you read too many of those supermarket tabloids. She looks like a woman in trouble to me."

"I'm warning you, George…"

Heedless of his wife's fears, George put his foot on the brake and the car slowed. He had decided he would slowly drive by the woman to see whether it was a ruse or she really needed help. He didn't want to pass her by and then have the thought sitting on his mind, keeping him awake at night, that he could have done something to help.

As the car moved closer to the woman, the Greens could see bruises and bad cuts on her face and arms.

"This is not some trap, Maggie. That woman's in trouble."

George stopped the car, quickly got out and went to the woman. "Are you all right?"

"Yes, yes, I'm fine. Thank you for stopping. A deer ran out in front of us. We swerved to miss it and my husband lost control of the car. We ended up down there in that deep ditch. My husband and our three-month-old daughter are in there. I'm pretty sure my husband is dead, but I know Elizabeth is still alive. Please help me get her out."

As George started sliding down the banks of the ditch, he called back to the woman, "Don't come down. You stay here with my wife. Get inside the car and stay warm."

When he got down to the overturned car, he noticed two people in the front seat but he paid no attention to them for the moment. He thought he could hear a child whimpering. He managed to get the back door open. He got down on his hands and knees and saw a baby in an infant's car seat. He took out his pocketknife and started cutting the straps that held her. Yes, she was alive. George wrapped his arms around the little girl and got to his feet. He started climbing back up the steep banks of the ditch to take the baby to her mother.

Puffing and panting, George finally got back up to the roadway. The mother was nowhere in sight. Maggie rolled down her window and said, "Is the baby alive?"

"Yes. Where's her mother? I told her to get in the car with you."

"I thought you saw her. She followed right along behind you down the ditch."

"Followed me…?"

George slipped and slid back down the steep ditch to look for the woman. When he got to the car, he once again got on his hands and knees and looked in. Yes, clearly there were two people in the front seat, a man and a woman. He felt for the man's pulse. Nothing there. He was dead.

Then George moved around to the other side of the car. He felt for the woman's pulse. Dead too. Then he looked closer. The red-headed woman strapped into the front seat was the same person who moments before had asked him for help.

The Fickle Finger of Fate

Olga was a mail-order bride. She had immigrated to New York City from Estonia and almost immediately went to Silver City, Colorado, to become the bride of Sam Higgins, a struggling gold and silver miner.

Many of these mail-order marriages remained loveless, but that was not the case with Olga and Sam. They fell in love almost at first sight. Although they wanted children, they were never able to have any. So Olga adopted a little stray terrier whom she named Lookout. She lavished all her motherly love on the frisky little puppy, and he repaid her with protection and devotion.

Living conditions at Silver City were rather primitive, but the couple made do as best they could. Even though they had few luxuries, Sam was determined to show Olga how much she meant to him. He bought her a beautiful wedding ring topped with two half-carat diamonds and set in the gold from the Silver City mine.

Olga's ring became the talk of the town. Everyone stopped by to admire it. Such luxury was unheard of in this section of the country. Olga never took off the ring and would oftentimes stop in the middle of her chores to watch the sunlight play on the beveled stones.

By the time Lookout was seventeen years old, his eyesight and hearing had diminished considerably. His behavior began to change also. He seemed to see and hear things that no one else could. Olga loved him even more in spite of his eccentricities.

That year, just as the aspen trees began to turn gold on the mountainsides, a wave of diphtheria struck Silver City. The little mining town was decimated. Among those who caught the contagious disease was Olga. Sam nursed her, and Lookout stayed by her side as she lay in the bed.

After six weeks, her heart stopped and she died.

She looked beautiful lying in state in the front room—as if she had never been ill. Sam had dressed her in her white wedding gown, and her ring sparkled in the candlelight. The mourners who arrived for the wake asked Sam about the ring. Was he going to take it off her finger before he buried her?

Sam looked at the questioners in amazement. "Take the ring off? Of course not! It was her most prized possession. She never took it off while she lived. I'll certainly not take it off her now."

She was buried the next afternoon in the old graveyard on the opposite side of town. As Sam trudged down the main street toward home, he had trouble holding Lookout in his arms. The little dog had not wanted to leave the gravesite, and Sam had been forced to pick him up and carry him home. All the way through town, Lookout whimpered and struggled to run back to his mistress's grave. Once they were home, Lookout jumped onto Olga's bed and howled pitifully.

By midnight that evening, the town was quiet except for a few men still drinking in Silver City's saloon. They were the first to hear the lonesome moaning. They dismissed it as the wind. But it persisted, becoming louder and more plaintive. Clearly someone or something was calling for help. Jake Witherspoon, one of the drunken men in the saloon, wobbled to the front window and looked out into the moonlit street. He gasped as he saw a figure that seemed to move toward him—a figure in a white dress.

"My God! My God, boys! It's Olga's ghost."

The other men stared at him drunkenly.

"You stupid old fool. You're seeing things!"

"Damn right I'm seeing things! It's the ghost of Olga, I'm telling you! Get my rifle, Willie. I'm gonna blow this shade to smithereens!"

The figure in the white dress continued to weave down the street moaning and crying. As it got closer to the saloon, the men could see a great deal of blood on the left side of her white dress.

Back at his cabin, Sam, sleeping in his chair, was awakened by Lookout's frenzied barking at the door.

"What is it, old boy? You hear a coyote?"

Sam moved to the door and opened it a crack. Lookout immediately shot through the opening and started running down Main Street. Just then Sam heard a gunshot. He ran after Lookout, calling him to come back.

"You missed, Jake, you drunken old fool," said Willie. "Here, give me the rifle. You couldn't hit a bull in the behind with a bass fiddle!"

Just as Willie raised the rifle to his shoulder, he saw a small dog race out of the darkness. It jumped into the arms of the apparition and began licking its face.

"That ain't no ghost. That's Olga for sure, back from the grave."

He threw down the rifle, and all the men began running toward Olga.

Sam reached Olga first, just as she slumped to the ground. He carried her inside the saloon and placed her on a pool table. The miners gathered around as her eyes began to flutter open. Sam gave her some water as Willie wrapped a blanket around her. Once she was fully conscious, Sam said, "Thank God you're alive! But how can it be? What happened?"

"I don't know. The last thing I remember I was lying in bed at home. I thought I'd just dropped off to sleep. Then there was a rush of fresh air that began to waken me. Suddenly I felt a sharp pain in my hand. I opened my eyes to see someone trying to cut off my finger—trying to get my diamond wedding ring."

"Who was it, Olga? Could you see?"

"Yes. It was Jake. Old Jake Witherspoon."

The men turned and looked at Jake, who had shrunk back into a corner of the saloon. The rifle that he had used to shoot at Olga was leveled in his direction.

"Better say your prayers, Jake. You're about as lowdown as they . . . "

"No, no," said Olga. "Don't do anything to him. Don't you understand? It was lucky for me that Jake tried to steal my ring! I would still be in that casket if he hadn't. He saved my life. Sam, give me your knife."

Olga opened the blade and pried out one of the diamonds from her ring, then placed it on a table in front of Jake. "Here, Jake," she said. "Maybe this stone will bring you half as much luck as it has brought me. Come on, Sam, let's go home."

Pumped Up

Sherry pulled into a gas station. She inserted her credit card in the slot at the pump and filled her gas tank. She then replaced the nozzle and started to get back in her car and leave. As she walked around the hood, she heard the attendant's voice over the loudspeaker. Something had happened with her credit card payment and she needed to come inside and re-pay.

Sherry was confused, because the transaction at the pump seemed complete and approved. She decided to ignore him. The attendant once again urged her to come inside to pay, this time saying that if she didn't he would be forced to call the authorities.

Sherry went inside and started arguing with the attendant about his threat. He told her to calm down and listen carefully.

"While you were pumping gas," he said, "I saw a guy slip into the back seat of your car from the other side. I've called the police."

She looked out in time to see the police pull up. She watched as they surrounded her car. With guns drawn, the cops opened the back doors and dragged a man wearing a ski mask from the back seat.

The police later informed her that this was a new gang initiation rite. The requirement was to bring back a woman's body part.

Listening to Your Parents

This actually happened to a friend of my dearest new friend's daughter.

Her daughter, Lauren, is nineteen years old and a sophomore in college. This happened to her over the Christmas/New Year's holiday break. It was the Saturday before New Year's and it was about one o'clock in the afternoon.

Lauren was driving from Winchester to visit a friend in Warrenton. For those of you who are familiar with the area, she was taking Route 50 East toward Middleburg and was then going to cut over to Route 66. Those of you who aren't familiar with this area--50 East is a main road (two lanes on each side with a big median separating the eastbound and westbound lanes), but is somewhat secluded, meaning mostly residences along the road rather than commercial businesses. Lauren was actually following behind a state police car shortly after she left Winchester and was going just over 65 MPH since she was following behind him.

An unmarked police car pulled up behind her and put his lights on. My friend and her husband have four children (high school and college age) and have always told them never to pull over for an unmarked car on the side of the road, but rather wait until they get to a gas station, etc. So Lauren had actually listened to her parents' advice, and promptly called #77 on her cell phone to tell the dispatcher that she would not pull over right away. She proceeded to tell the dispatcher that there were two police cars, one unmarked behind her and one marked in front of her.

The dispatcher checked if there were two police cars where she was. There weren't. The dispatcher connected her to the policeman in front of her, and he told her to keep driving and remain calm. He already had backup on the way.

Five minutes later four cop cars surrounded her and the unmarked car behind her.

One policeman went to her side and the others surrounded the car behind her. They pulled the driver from the car and tackled him to the ground. It turned out the man was a convicted rapist and wanted for other crimes. Thank God Lauren listened to her parents! She was shaken up, but fine.

I never knew that bit of advice, but especially for a woman alone in a car, you should *not* pull over for an unmarked car in a secluded area. In fact, even a marked car should follow you to a populated area after dark. Police officers have to respect your right to keep going to a "safe" place. You obviously need to make some signals that you acknowledge them, i.e., put on your hazard lights or call #77 like Lauren did. I am so thankful that my friend was just sitting at our book club meeting telling us this scary story, rather than us at her house consoling her.

Be safe and pass this on to your friends. Awareness is everything.

Earthworms

In the 1960s, the price of beef of went up so high the fast-food chains decided to use earthworms as filler in the beef. The FDA allowed it since nothing in earthworms is harmful to humans. A few years later, the price of commercially produced earthworms got so high the restaurants could no longer afford to mix them with the beef, so they stopped using them. These days they're looking into the possibility of using maggots as filler—they are high in protein, low in fat, and extremely cheap to reproduce.

Wooden You? Wooden We?

A number of fake airfields were built during World War II to mislead the enemy into making useless bombing runs. The Germans set up one such decoy field in occupied Holland. It was constructed entirely of wood and canvas—wood and canvas airplane hangers, wood and canvas oil tanks, wood and canvas gun turrets, wood and canvas trucks, even wood and canvas airplanes.

At last the day came when every aspect of the decoy field was complete. The Germans were pleased that the Allied Forces would waste precious bombs on this fake target they had erected ... but there was one slight hitch. In their thoroughness, the Germans had taken so long to build this fake airfield that Allied photo planes had had plenty of opportunities to fly over and document exactly what was going on. The very next day, a lone RAF Hurricane flew over the English Channel to the Dutch coast. It stayed low to avoid radar detection and arrived at the fake wood and canvas airfield. The Hurricane circled the field then—making a direct pass over it—opened the bomb bay doors and dropped a load of wood and canvas bombs.

Hoax!

The senior consultant of a large northwestern timber company received a telephone call from a man identifying himself as an AT&T service technician who was conducting a test on the telephone lines. He told the consultant to complete the test by touching nine (9), zero (0), the pound sign (#) and then hanging up.

The consultant was suspicious and refused. When he contacted the telephone company, the service representative told him that if he had pushed 90#, he would have given the connected party full access to his telephone line, enabling him to place long-distance calls on his account. He was further informed that this scam had originated from local jails and prisons. He also verified this information with UCB Telecom, Pacific Bell, MCI, Bell Atlantic, and GTE.

Hitler Clones

During the dark days toward the end of the Cold War, the Soviet Union was looking for a weapon that would guarantee its world dominance. Somehow, the KGB had acquired Adolf Hitler's bloody handkerchief found at Eagle's Nest, the bunker in Bavaria where he died in 1945.

The Soviets began experiments to clone new Adolf Hitlers following the amazing discovery by James Watson and Francis Crick in 1953 of deoxyribonucleic acid, DNA. Watson and Crick had observed how DNA's "double helix" structure could "unzip" to make copies of itself. Using the DNA from Hitler's bloody handkerchief, the Soviets were able to successfully clone six hundred Hitlers. These human clones were reared by Russian families and indoctrinated with Soviet ideals. When the Soviet Union began to dissolve in the early '90s, the Russians realized this project was too dangerous to continue without central government supervision. As a result, all the young Hitler clones were rounded up and put in a secret detention center in Siberia.

Even today, the Russians are trying to decide what to do with these Hitler clones. The most disturbing aspect of this whole operation, however, is that twenty-five of the clones have escaped and are now somewhere in the world. No one knows where they are or what they are doing.

If you are one of these clones, call immediately: 1-800-ACHTUNG.

Drops in the Bucket

A stock clerk was sent to clean up a storeroom in Honolulu, Hawaii. When he returned to the floor, he complained that the storeroom was filthy and that he had noticed dried mouse or rat droppings in some areas.

A couple of days later, the clerk began to feel like he was coming down with a stomach flu. He complained of sore joints and headaches and began to vomit. He went to bed and never really got up again. Within two days he was severely ill and weak. His blood sugar count was down to 66, and his face and eyeballs were yellow. He was rushed to the emergency room at Pali Momi, where he was diagnosed with massive organ failure. He died shortly before midnight.

No one would have made the connection between his job and his death, had it not been for a doctor who specifically asked if he had been in a warehouse or exposed to dried rat or mouse droppings at any time. The doctor identified a virus (much like the Hanta virus) that lives in dried rodent droppings. Once dried, these droppings are like dust and can easily be breathed in or ingested if a person does not wear protective gear or fails to wash face and hands thoroughly.

The investigation of soda cans by the Center for Disease Control in Atlanta determined that the tops of soda cans can be encrusted with dried rat's urine, which is so toxic it can be lethal. Canned drinks and other foodstuffs are stored in warehouses and containers that are usually infested with rodents, and then they get transported to retail outlets without being properly cleaned.

The autopsy performed on the clerk confirmed the doctor's suspicions. This is why it is extremely important to *always* carefully rinse off the tops of canned sodas or foods, and to wipe off pasta packaging, cereal boxes, and other containers.

Almost everything you buy in a supermarket was stored in a warehouse at one time or another. Most of us remember to wash vegetables and fruits but never think of boxes and cans. The ugly truth is, even the most modern, upscale superstore has rats and mice. And their warehouse most assuredly does!

Whenever you buy any canned soft drink, please make sure that you wash the top with running water and soap or, if that is not available, drink with a straw.

Made in USA

In the years following World War II, Japan struggled to rebuild its devastated country, as well as its manufacturing capabilities, by producing large amounts of cheap goods for export to countries all over the world. Following the war, the United States was blessed with a strong economy and bought much of the world's goods. It was the primary target for Japan's export business. To Americans, however, the phrase "Made in Japan" soon came to mean anything that was cheaply and poorly made. The Japanese, ever sensitive to bad publicity, started funneling all their exports through a city on the island of Shokoku—the city of Usa. By doing this, they could truthfully say that their products were "Made in USA."

Boom, Boom, Big Birdie

At a time when the French were developing their new high-speed bullet trains, they heard about tests being conducted by the Federal Aeronautics Administration in the United States. The FAA was testing not only how safely jet engines could ingest a bird in flight, but also the strength of the cockpit windows if they were hit by a large bird. They had rigged a modified cannon that could shoot objects at approximately 650 miles per hour, roughly the same speed as a cruising jetliner. The ammo used by the FAA were dead chickens purchased from the local supermarket, their thought being that if the cockpit window could stay intact after being hit by a dead chicken, it would survive being hit by a live bird as well.

The French thought this would be a good test for the trains they were developing. They contacted the FAA authorities and arranged to have a chicken cannon shipped over to them. When it arrived, the French set it up, loaded the launcher and let it rip. The poultry projectile proceeded to shatter the train's windshield, ripped through the engineer's chair, and demolished the instrument panel behind it. The French testers immediately called the FAA and demanded an explanation. After the French test had been reviewed by the FAA, they called the French bullet train manufacturer and said, "Next time, before you shoot the chicken out of the cannon, thaw it first."

The French did and, during the lunch break, a cat, attracted by the aroma of fresh chicken, climbed into the launcher … and became part of the test as well.

For All You Engineers Out There

(or, For Want of A Nail...)

The U.S. standard railroad gauge (width between the two rails) is 4 feet, 8.5 inches. That's an exceedingly odd number. Why was that gauge used? Because that's the way they built them in England, and the U.S. railroads were built by English expatriates. Why did the English build them like that? Because theirs were the first rail lines and that's the gauge they used.

Why then did *they* use that gauge? Because the people who built the tramways used the same jigs and tools that they used for building wagons, which used the same wheel spacing.

Why did the wagons have that particular odd wheel spacing? Well, if they tried to use any other spacing, the wagon wheels would break on some of the old, long-distance roads in England, because that's the spacing of the wheel ruts.

So who built those old rutted roads? The first long-distance roads in England (and much of Europe) were built by Imperial Rome for their legions. The roads have been used ever since those ancient days. And the ruts in the roads? Roman war chariots first formed the initial ruts, which everyone else had to match for fear of destroying their wagon wheels. Since the chariots were made for (or by) Imperial Rome, they were all alike in the matter of wheel spacing.

The United States standard railroad gauge of 4 feet, 8.5 inches derives from the original specification for an Imperial Roman war chariot. Specifications and bureaucracies live forever. So the next time you are handed a specification and wonder what horse's ass came up with it, you may be exactly right, because the Imperial Roman war chariots were made just wide enough to accommodate the back ends of two war horses. Thus, we have the answer to the original question.

Now the twist to the story.

When we see a space shuttle sitting on its launch pad, there are two big booster rockets attached to the sides of the main fuel tank. These are solid rocket boosters, or SRBs. The SRBs are made by Thiokol at their factory in Utah. The engineers who designed the SRBs might have preferred to make them a bit fatter, but the SRBs had to be shipped by train from the factory to the launch site. The railroad line from the factory had to run through a tunnel in the mountains. The SRBs had to fit through that tunnel. The tunnel is slightly wider than the railroad track, and the railroad track is about as wide as two horses' behinds.

So, the major design feature of what is arguably the world's most advanced transportation system was determined over two thousand years ago by the width of a horse's ass!

Hang in There, Bob!

Bob was known to be a great practical joker. His new wife, Lynn, knew about his reputation and demanded that he give up these childish pranks and never play a practical joke on her. Reluctantly, he promised to stop.

Shortly after Bob and Lynn moved into a new apartment complex, they noticed that their superintendent, a seemingly sweet gray-haired woman, was always going in and out of their neighbors' apartments during the day. Bob wondered if she was snooping around in their place as well. They soon began to notice that several small items were missing—cufflinks, earrings, even some expensive wine glasses.

After a bottle of Bob's finest wine disappeared, he knew he had to put a stop to the super's visits. Without telling his wife, he devised a plan. He brought home a long rope, which he tied in a hangman's noose. Then, using leather straps, he constructed a harness that would safely support him while making it appear that he had hanged himself from a living room rafter.

One morning after Lynn had left for work, Bob rigged the noose and harness, climbed on a chair, and attached it to a rafter. Then he got into the harness, kicked the chair away, and waited. Soon he heard a key in the lock. He closed his eyes and pretended to be dead. He heard the door open, followed by a gasp and a heavy thud. He opened his eyes to see his wife lying on the floor. She had come back home to pick up a report she had forgotten to take that morning. Seeing her husband hanging from the rafter had caused her to faint.

As Bob started to unstrap the harness to get down and help her, he heard footsteps in the hallway and suspected it might be the super. He pretended to be dead again. Looking through his eyelashes, Bob watched the super bend down to feel Lynn's pulse. Then he saw her take off Lynn's gold necklace. She did not try to help his wife, nor did she phone the police or the emergency squad. Instead, she headed straight for the sideboard and threw Lynn's expensive silverware into a plastic garbage bag. The super then ran down the hall to the bedroom and snatched all the jewelry from the dresser. As she started toward the front door, the super grabbed an expensive painting off the wall. This was too much for Bob. As she passed by his swinging body, he kicked her rear end as hard as he could and yelled, "You miserable thief!"

The shock of being kicked by a dead man caused the super to go into immediate cardiac arrest. The silverware and jewelry spilled out on the carpet as she crumpled to the floor, dead.

Speed Bumps

Fred and Marge had spent years planning a trip to Central America once Fred retired. They planned to drive from their home in Los Angeles in a brand new RV outfitted for the trip. Their friends tried to discourage them, telling them bandits and outlaws hid out in the remote regions of Mexico. An old couple in a fancy travel home would make an inviting target.

Fred and Marge were not about to give up their dream. They equipped their RV with a powerful engine, an extra large gas tank, and all-terrain knobby tires. Fred also bought himself a .44 magnum for the trip.

Everything went well until they reached the mountains a hundred miles south of Mexico City. Driving on a lonely stretch of highway one evening, they saw a car parked across the two-lane road, blocking traffic. All the doors were open, and no one was in sight. Fred told Marge it looked like a bandits' set up and to hold on. Without slowing down, he headed off the road into the tall grass on the right shoulder, dodging the car. They began to hear shouts behind them. Fred floored it, sure that the robbers were trying to jump them. The roadside was particularly rough and bumpy. He felt the RV tilt dangerously, but he managed to hold it upright, with his foot still heavy on the accelerator.

He swerved back on to the blacktop and raced toward the nearest town, ten miles away. When he pulled up at the police station, he told the captain what had happened. The captain asked Fred and Marge to help him find the place where the attempted robbery occurred. Much to their amazement, the car was still parked across the road when they returned. Pistols drawn, they got out to investigate. They could find nothing until they walked over to the grassy roadside where Fred had swerved around the car.

Following the RV tracks, they were dumb-struck to see six banditos, lying on their stomachs, their AK-47s still pointing toward the road—their crushed lifeless bodies showing the deep imprint of the RV's knobby tires.

Arrested Development

A young man walked into a liquor store carrying a sawed-off shotgun and demanded all the money from the cash register. While the clerk was putting the money in a plastic bag, the robber saw a bottle of scotch whiskey and handed it to him.

"Here, Buddy, put this scotch in the bag as well."

"I'm sorry, sir, but I can't do that."

"Can't…? Why not?"

"Because I don't believe you are twenty-one."

"I'm twenty-one! I'm over twenty-one."

"Well, you're going to have to prove it to me."

Exasperated, the robber took his driver's license out of his wallet and slammed it on the counter.

"There! See? I'm almost twenty-two!"

The clerk examined the license. Agreeing that the robber was over twenty-one, he put the bottle of scotch in the bag.

As the young man ran from the store with his loot, the clerk promptly called the police and gave them the name and address he found on the license.

They arrested the robber two hours later.

The Lights Are On, but No One's Home

(or, Stupid Criminal Tricks)

A couple of robbers went into a liquor store in central Illinois, nervously waving their pistols.

"Don't nobody move!" shouted the taller of the two bandits.

When his partner reached for the cash register, the tall bandit shot him.

***

A guy decided to rob a liquor store. He tried the door but it was locked. This made him angry, so he picked up a cinder block and heaved it over his head at the front window. The cinder block bounced back and hit the hapless thief on the head, knocking him out cold. It seems the liquor store window was shatterproof Plexiglas. The security cameras caught the whole thing on videotape, which is now played endlessly on reality TV.

***

A man walked into an all-night Burger King in eastern Nebraska at 3:50 A.M., pulled out a gun, and demanded cash.

"I'm sorry, sir," said the clerk, "but I can't open the cash register without a food order."

"All right, then," said the thief, "give me an order of onion rings to go."

"I'm sorry, sir, but onion rings are not available for breakfast."

Frustrated, the thief said, "Fuggeddaboutit!" and walked away.

***

In California, a man attempted to hold up a Bank of America branch. He was unarmed, but used his thumb and finger to simulate a gun. Unfortunately, he forgot to keep his hand in his pocket.

OCCUPATIONAL HAZARDS

Hit or Miss

A young intern was leaving the office late one evening when he found the company's chief executive officer standing in front of a shredder with a piece of paper in his hand, looking puzzled.

"Listen, son," said the CEO. "This is a very sensitive and important document here, and my secretary has gone for the night. Can you make this thing work for me?"

"Certainly," said the young intern, pleased to have a chance to impress the boss. He turned the machine on, inserted the paper, and pressed the start button.

"Excellent, excellent!" said the CEO, as his paper disappeared inside the machine. "I just need one copy..."

Take a Meeting, Take a Hike

Mick Jagger was dining at Patina Restaurant in Santa Monica when a young talent agent interrupted his meal.

"Excuse me, Mr. Jagger, I know this is a great imposition, but could you do me a big favor? I've got a client with me who I really need to impress, and he thinks I don't know any big celebrities. Could you just stop by my table on your way out and say 'Hi, Biff, how's it going?'"

Jagger agreed to do it.

As he was leaving, he passed the young man's table. "Great to see you, Biff," he said. "How's life treating you?"

The young agent gave him a look of exasperation. "Oh, Mick, stop being such a pest! Can't you see I'm taking an important meeting?"

The Blind Man

Two young nuns had been detailed to paint a room in the convent. The weather had been ferociously hot for several weeks. After an hour or so, the nun's habits were soaked, so they decided, to take them off, and everything under them. They locked the door and stripped down.

They were about half-finished with the painting when they heard a knock at the door. "Who is it?" one of the nuns called out.

"The blind man," came the reply.

"Should we let him in?"

"Well, he said he was blind."

"True. Then we wouldn't have to put our hot sweaty habits back on."

They went to the door and opened it. A man stood here holding a large package. He looked at the two nude nuns and said, "Where would you like these window blinds hung?"

You're Driving Me Crazy

The wealthy owner of a large manufacturing plant in the Midwest had imported a famous French chef, who went by the single name of Napoleon, to run his executive dining room. His food soon became famous throughout the region. The businessman was on the board of trustees of a nearby university. The president persuaded him to donate Napoleon's services for a fancy dinner for potential million-dollar donors.

When he was preparing to leave, Napoleon couldn't find his knife satchel, so he wrapped the sharp blades in a piece of old newspaper and got in his car. The car wouldn't start. Napoleon was already late for his job at the university, so he went back in his house and phoned a cab. The dispatcher told him all their cabs were spoken for and he couldn't send one for at least an hour. Napoleon then remembered the bus that went past his house.

He just caught the bus and, breathing heavily, shouted at the driver, "Step on zee gas, monsieur, zee president is waiting pour moi!"

The bus driver looked at Napoleon, then looked at the carving knives wrapped in newspaper. "It's your call, pal," he replied, and drove him directly to the state insane asylum.

Seeing all the institutional-type buildings, Napoleon thought, *This must be the university*. As he approached the guard at the gate, he unwrapped his knives and said, "I am Napoleon! Take me to zee prezident!"

The next thing Napoleon knew, he was in a padded cell. It took Napoleon's boss about eight hours to get him released. Napoleon immediately went back to France where "zee peepuls are not zo crazee!"

"Special" Delivery

FBI agents were detailed to investigate allegations of fraud committed by a company that operated thirteen psychiatric hospitals in a five-state region. In a coordinated raid, the agents broke into the business offices of all thirteen hospitals on a Sunday morning. The raid at one of the hospitals turned into an all-day affair. Around two in the afternoon, the FBI agent-in-charge started getting hungry and called a local pizza joint.

"Hello, Vinnie's Pizza. Whaddaya need?"

"I'd like five large pizzas. Two plain. Two with sausage. And one with pepperoni."

"Yeah, OK. Where're they to go?"

"Bellewood Psychiatric Hospital."

"Bellewood?"

"That's correct."

"Who's calling?

"I'm with the FBI."

"You saying you're an FBI agent?"

"Affirmative. All of us here are."

"FBI agents."

"Affirmative."

"And you're all at Bellewood Psychiatric Hospital?"

"Affirmative. When you deliver the pizzas, don't go to the front door. We have that locked. Go around to the service entrance."

"You're all FBI agents?"

"Affirmative."

"And you're all at Bellewood?"

"Affirmative. How soon do you think you can deliver them?"

"You say everyone at Bellewood today is an FBI agent?"

"Affirmative. We're starving."

"And you're all FBI agents?"

"Affirmative. I told you that. Oh, and bring a case of cold Cokes. Remember, don't try the front doors. They're locked. Come around back."

"I don't freaking think so."

And the pizzeria's phone went dead.

NYPD Blue

Detective Sergeant Charlie Rumple and his partner, Detective Ivor Petersen, of the mid-Manhattan precinct, were sent to investigate a suicide on East Forty-seventh Street. The suicide was a "jumper" whose body had been caught by a net put up at the eighth floor to discourage such things. The net had done its job, but, oddly enough, the suicide victim was dead—not from the fall but from a shotgun blast to his head. Since he would normally have survived, a murder investigation was begun.

At the same time, detectives Rumple and Petersen received a phone call forwarded to them from a woman on the fifteenth floor of this same building who reported she had heard a gunshot coming from apartment #1522—the one right next to hers. As the two detectives knocked on the door of #1522, they heard shouting and angry words coming from inside. When the door was opened, the detectives found an old man and woman squabbling. The man was holding a twelve-gauge shotgun. The argument raged around who had loaded the gun.

It turned out the old couple argued a lot, and each argument ended with the old man pointing an unloaded shotgun at his wife and pulling the trigger. This time, however, the gun had been loaded. The blast had missed the wife, shattered their fifteenth-floor window, and evidently blown away the head of the suicide jumper as he fell.

The old man swore up and down he never kept the gun loaded—it had not been loaded in years. The only other person who had been in their apartment all day was their son, and he had left an hour earlier. Rumple and Petersen went to question the son but could not locate him.

Further investigation by the police department revealed that the jumper, Bobby Vargas, had been experiencing severe financial setbacks. His credit was maxxed out, and his parents had cut off his funding. Rumple and Petersen, through continued probing, discovered that Vargas's parents lived on the fifteenth floor of the same building from which he had jumped. The old couple having the argument were, in fact,

Bobby's parents.

Aware of his parents' tendency to argue at the drop of a hat, as well as the old man's dramatics with an unloaded gun, Bobby had secretly loaded the shotgun, knowing that sooner or later his father would threaten his mother with it, and pull the trigger. Then, with his mother dead and his father in jail, Bobby stood to inherit all of their considerable wealth.

It turned out that earlier in the morning Bobby had indeed been in his parents' apartment. He had begged them to loan him the money to cover his debts but they refused. Disconsolate, he went up on the roof of his parents' apartment house and, an hour later, decided to punish them for their stinginess by jumping to his death. During the hour that Bobby spent on the roof, his father and mother had argued furiously about whether their son should be given the money, and true to form, old man Vargas got out the shotgun, pointed it at his wife, and pulled the trigger. Seconds before the old man pulled the trigger, however, Bobby had flung himself from the roof. The shotgun blast missed Mrs. Vargas, shattered the apartment window, and then struck their son in the head as he sailed by, killing him instantly.

After prolonged debate, the coroner's office ruled it was death by misadventure, since for all practical purposes, Bobby Vargas had killed himself. At the 1994 National Conference of City Coroners, this event was named the most innovative death of the year. The story was sold to television but was never produced because the network executives felt viewers would find it too unbelievable.

Oh, Deer Me!

There is no doubt about it. Harry was intoxicated. His "one for the road" was at least three too many. As he drove out of town to his farm five miles away, the car weaved from one side of the road to the other.

Just as Harry made a sharp turn to the left, a deer jumped onto the road and hit the car. When he finally got the car stopped, Harry hopped out and staggered back to the animal lying in the road. He examined the deer and decided that its neck was broken. Not wanting a good deer to go to waste, Harry backed up the car, opened the back door and—lifting, pulling, shoving—loaded the deer into the back seat and continued on his way.

The deer, however, was not dead—only stunned. Finding itself in the back seat of a moving automobile was definitely not something it was accustomed to. In short order, the deer began kicking and thrashing. It bit Harry on the neck. If Harry's driving was erratic before, it now became hysterical. He plowed through a barbed wire fence, over a field, and onto another road. Soon, he had no idea where he was.

Up ahead, Harry saw a general store with a lighted phone booth beside it. He pulled up, hurtled out of the car, opened the trunk, and got out a knife and a tire iron. As he started to open the back door of the car to subdue the thrashing deer, a large guard dog came running out from behind the store and bit Harry on the leg. He tried desperately to fend off the hostile dog with the knife and tire iron, all the time looking for a safe place. He couldn't get back in the car; the deer was still kicking and writhing, wreaking havoc inside the car with its antlers and hooves. Then he spied the phone booth.

Harry moved as quickly as he could to the booth and slammed the door, bracing it with his foot. The dog leapt against the glass, trying to get at Harry. Rivulets of saliva ran down the door. Harry frantically picked up the receiver and dialed 911 while the guard dog pounded the glass of the phone booth, trying to get in.

"Emergency operator. How can I help you?"

"Ambulance!" screamed Harry. "Send an ambulance now!"

"What is your location?"

"Location …?"

Harry had no idea where he was. He saw that the dog's attention has shifted to the deer in the back seat of the car. He darted out of the phone booth, looking for a landmark or signage that would help him describe his location to the emergency operator. The dog saw him and came after him again. Harry barely made it back to the phone booth. *The general store must have a name*, he thought. Once again he ventured out. Once more the dog came after him, but not before Harry had seen the name on a sign.

"Switzer's General Store!" he shouted into the phone.

"What is the nature of the accident, sir?" asked the emergency operator.

When Harry finished recounting what had happened to him within the past five minutes, the emergency operator coldly replied, "Sir, do you realize it is a federal offense to phone in a false alarm as you have just done? I've a good mind to tell the police about you." Harry heard a loud click, followed by the dial tone.

Mysteries of the Deep

Tara Lee was one of the most popular girls in high school, and during her senior year she was elected prom queen. Her proud parents agreed to send her to Cancun over spring break as an early graduation present. The Mexican resort was filled with young students determined to have a good time. Tara Lee's days were spent snorkeling and swimming in the Gulf. Her nights were spent partying and having as much fun as could be crammed into the eight-day vacation.

Later on in May, she graduated with honors. Shortly after graduation, however, her stomach began to swell. She was bothered by nausea every morning. Her mother soon noticed her illness and her swelling belly.

"We trusted you to go down to Cancun and have a good time. We didn't expect you to come back pregnant!"

"I'm *not* pregnant, Mother. I've never been with a boy in my life!"

"Then how do you explain this condition?"

"I don't know. I can't."

"We're going to the doctor, young lady, and right now!"

Tara Lee was examined, tested and, finally, X-rayed.

"This isn't a baby," said the doctor. "It looks like a tumor. We need to operate immediately."

The medical staff in the operating room was astounded when they opened her up and found not a baby, not a tumor, but an eight-pound octopus. Its slimy tentacles were suctioned tightly to the wall of her stomach.

On investigation, they discovered that Tara Lee had swallowed some of the thousands of microscopic octopus eggs that float on top of the seawater. One of the eggs had lodged in her stomach and hatched. It was well on its way to engulfing her whole body.

Shortcuts to Papercuts

A clerk in a Los Angeles post office noticed a letter was not properly sealed, so she quickly licked the envelope flap with her tongue and closed it. Normally she used a wet sponge to do a job like that, but this day she was distracted. She felt a slight stinging sensation at the time and assumed the envelope flap had given her tongue a paper cut.

A couple of days later, her tongue began to swell. It was not sore, but she was having trouble pronouncing words. She made an appointment with her doctor, but he found nothing wrong. After two more days, her tongue had swollen larger, and now it began to hurt. It was so sore she could not eat. She went back to her doctor who, after he took an X-ray of her tongue, saw a lump that needed removing. He prepared her for minor surgery. When the doctor cut her tongue open, a live roach crawled out.

Roach eggs had been embedded in the seal of the envelope. The eggs were able to hatch inside of her tongue because her saliva kept them warm and moist. The doctor had to remove about half her tongue.

Now she tells all her customers, "Ahwayth uth a wet thponge to theal a letteth!"

Guns and MRIs Don't Mix

That's what an off-duty Rochester cop found out this week when he went to a clinic for a Magnetic Resonance Imaging test. The cop told a clinic worker he had his handgun with him.

The worker told him it was OK to keep it. But as soon as the cop entered the room, the device's heavy-duty magnet yanked the .45-caliber gun right out of his hand. When the gun hit the magnet, a bullet was fired. The bullet lodged in a wall, and no one was hurt. The MRI device, however, refused to let go of the gun. It took three hours to power down the magnet and release the weapon.

An MRI is four times as powerful as magnets used to lift cars in junkyards, said Sgt. William Benwitz, who runs a firearms training unit for the Rochester police force. Benwitz said it would be too risky to try firing the weapon, because its molecular structure might have been altered.

"Until we send this gun back to the factory, we're not even going to test-fire it," he said. "The metal is more brittle than it should be."

Me? Drunk?

From Texas, where drinking and driving are sometimes considered a sporting event, comes the true story that happened to a friend of a friend of mine.

A patrol car was routinely parked outside a neighborhood bar. Late in the evening, the policeman noticed a man leaving the bar so intoxicated that he could barely walk. The man stumbled around the parking lot for several minutes with the officer quietly watching him. After thirty or forty minutes—the man trying his keys in eight different vehicles—he managed to find his own car, which he promptly fell into. He slumped over the steering wheel for a few minutes as a number of other patrons left the bar and drove away.

He finally started his car, switched on the windshield wipers (even though it was a clear night), clicked the hazard flasher on and off, tooted the horn, and then pulled on the headlights. He drove the car forward a few feet, reversed a little and then remained stationary for a few more minutes as other bar patrons drove away. At last, when his was the only car left, he pulled out of the bar's parking lot and started to drive slowly down the street.

The police officer, having patiently waited all this time, now started up his patrol car and put on the flashing lights. He promptly pulled the man over and administered a breathalyzer test. To his amazement, the breathalyzer indicated no evidence that the man had consumed alcohol at all! Dumbfounded, the officer said, "I'll have to ask you to come with me to the station house. This breathalyzer equipment must be broken."

"I doubt it," said the man. "Tonight I'm the designated decoy."

You Can Bank On It

A woman walked into a bank in New York City and asked for the loan officer. She explained that she was going to Europe on business for two weeks and needed to borrow $5,000. Her credit checked out, but the officer explained the bank would need some kind of security for the loan. She dug in her purse and handed over the keys to a new Rolls Royce parked on the street in front of the bank. The bank agreed to accept the car as collateral for the loan.

The bank's president and its officers all enjoyed a good laugh at the woman for using a $250,000 Rolls as collateral against a $5,000 loan. An employee of the bank then proceeded to drive the Rolls into the bank's underground garage and park it there.

Two weeks later, the woman returned and repaid the $5,000 and the interest, which amounted to $15.41. The loan officer said, "Miss, we are very happy to have had your business, and this transaction has worked out very nicely, but we are a little puzzled. While you were away, we checked you out and found that you are a multimillionaire. What puzzles us is, why would you bother to borrow $5000?"

"Young man," she replied, "Where else in New York can I park my car for two weeks for only $15.41?"

Simple Gifts

When the New York City garbage workers went on strike in the summer of 1975, one enterprising New Yorker did not let it get him down. Each evening he would put his garbage in a cardboard box and tape it closed. Then he wrapped it neatly in gift paper. After that, he put the gift-wrapped refuse in a shopping bag and left it on the front seat of his car with the window rolled down. When he came back thirty minutes later—*voila!*—his garbage had been collected.

Rolling, Rolling, Rolling

Morris had been employed by the local factory for thirty-five years, never once missing a day of work. Each evening after his shift he would push a wheelbarrow loaded with straw to the front gate. The guard would dutifully search through the straw, find nothing, and allow Morris to pass through.

The day Morris retired he walked to the front gate, but this time without a wheelbarrow. The guard again stopped him and said, "Morris, I've checked you every night for the past three and a half decades. Now, I know you've been stealing something, but for the life of me I can't figure out what it is. It's been driving me crazy. Now that you're retired, why don't you let me in on your secret. I promise not to tell anyone. What is it you've been stealing?"

Morris was silent for a moment. Then, with a smile, he said, "Wheelbarrows."

Smokey Hokel

Harvey was the best mason in town. His fireplaces were highly prized. They were not only beautiful works of art, but they were designed to reliably draw the smoke up the chimney. Horace Wainwright, the wealthiest man in town, had contracted Harvey to build him a fancy fireplace. Harvey had been warned that Mr. Wainwright was a terrible cheapskate and would try to skin him out of the money.

When Harvey finished the job, he went to get his money; but Mr. Wainwright said he couldn't pay just now.

"Oh, that's all right," said Harvey. "But if I have to wait for my money then you have to wait to use your fireplace."

Mr. Wainwright agreed. He wouldn't build a fire in the fireplace until he had paid Harvey all he was owed.

A couple of hours after Harvey arrived home, he received a frantic phone call from Mr. Wainwright.

"Get your tail over here right now, young man! My house is full of smoke!"

"I don't know why it should be. You didn't start a fire in the fireplace, did you?"

"Yes, I did."

"But we agreed you wouldn't use the fireplace until I had been paid in full."

"I know! I know! Look, I'll pay you. I'll give you a bonus. Just get over here and fix my fireplace!"

Once Harvey had the full payment in hand, he climbed up to the roof carrying a brick. He dropped the brick down the chimney. There was a loud crash—the sound of shattering glass. Harvey had mortared a pane of glass across the flue to ensure he would be paid in full.

Slavemaster

Kathy Gruninger sat nodding at her home computer as she surfed the Internet. Even though she was tired from her long day's work as a detective sergeant on the Charlottesville, Virginia, Police Department, she felt duty-bound to continue looking for new information about a disturbing urban legend called "Slavemaster." It had recently resurfaced as an e-mail warning to women. They should not open, much less read or answer anything sent to them from "Slavemaster." Supposedly, someone using that name was contacting women through the Internet, then torturing and killing them in gruesome ways.

Kathy's search for Slavemaster was not part of her job as a detective sergeant. The police were involved in far too many local cases to worry about some Internet crazy. That, however, did not deter Kathy's firm dedication to find and eradicate all hate crimes against women. Her first encounter with the Slavemaster story occurred during her undergraduate days at the university when she studied urban legends in a sociology class.

Now, finding little information other than what she already knew, Kathy left a message on a number of chatroom bulletin boards that she was looking for anything having to do with the Slavemaster story. Most of what she received just regurgitated the same old stuff, but Friday, she received an e-mail from someone named Charlie Spenser saying that

101

he had information she might find interesting. Kathy thought, *Could this be our sicko? Maybe I'm the bait that lured him out of his hole.* She wrote back to Charlie Spenser that she would be at her computer that evening—could they chat then?

Charlie contacted her at nine-thirty on Friday. He was sorry to be so late but he'd just got home from work. They chatted back and forth, discussing the fact that there was more than a grain of truth to the Slavemaster urban legend. Several years earlier, an Internet stalker in Olathe, Kansas, had used that name and ended up murdering eleven women he'd first met in chatrooms. Kathy asked Charlie what kind of work he did that kept him out so late. Charlie replied that he was a real estate agent, and it was because of that that he had answered her request. He then told Kathy about a rowhouse he was selling that had a very troubling addition.

According to Charlie, the house had been empty for some time. Purportedly, the owner had vanished without a trace, so the house had been repossessed by the mortgage company. Charlie, sensing a good business opportunity, bought the house for what was owed on the mortgage, hoping that he could turn it for a quick profit. When he had it inspected prior to putting it up for sale, he had discovered a trap door embedded in the floor of the downstairs hall closet. When he pulled open the trap door, he found, built underneath the foundation of the house, a six-by-six foot concrete dungeon with chains and wrist shackles attached to the walls.

Kathy let out a low whistle. "No wonder you thought it might have something to do with Slavemaster," she said. "Did you contact the police?"

"No, I didn't."

"Why not?"

"Frankly, I want to get my money out of it as quickly as I can. If a potential buyer ever found out this house had a dungeon underneath it, he'd walk away as fast as he could."

"Where is the place located?"

"Richmond," said Charlie, "Richmond, Virginia. That's where I sell real estate. The house is in the Fan district. You know, in all our talk, you've never told me why you're so interested in this Slavemaster."

For a moment, Kathy debated whether or not she should tell him that she was a police officer. After all, this wasn't official police business. So she said, "My major is folklore, but I'm specializing in urban legends like the Slavemaster story. I'm working on an advanced degree at UVA here in Charlottesville."

"UVA, huh?" said Charlie, "Wow, small world! I got my bachelor's at UVA more years ago than I care to admit. Say, I have an idea! Would you like to take a look at the house? It might be something you could include in your thesis. Maybe take photographs? I've got some workmen coming in Monday next week to fill in the hole and put in new flooring. But if you could make it over to Richmond before the work starts, I'd be happy to show you the place."

Charlie sounded so accommodating. Was he luring her or was he genuinely nice? She said, sure, she'd love to see the house. How about tomorrow? Charlie checked his appointment book and said that two-thirty in the afternoon would be a good time. He had a five o'clock house showing, so that should give Kathy plenty of time to look around and photograph the place if she wanted to. Deciding that she needed to get a read on him before she went to the house, she said, "Why don't we meet for lunch first, then go over to the house? That is, if you've got time."

Charlie said he did, and suggested a place where they should meet for lunch. Before Kathy signed off, she asked him what real estate firm he worked for. She was going to call them and check him out.

Saturday morning, when Kathy phoned them, they said, Yes, Charlie had been with the firm twelve years. He was one of their best agents. Would she like to leave a voicemail? Relieved, Kathy said no, she was just checking—for a friend. She then called her partner on the police force to let him know where she would be. He wasn't home, so Kathy left a message that she was going up to Richmond to see a real estate agent named Charlie Spenser. He had given her a lead about Slavemaster. If he hadn't heard from her by four o'clock he should come to the address he had given her.

When she met him at the restaurant, Charlie turned out to be a rather ordinary-looking guy who seemed pleasant enough, but rather shy—definitely not what she had expected. After they ordered lunch, Kathy tried to find out more about him, but he seemed reluctant to talk about himself.

After lunch, as they were leaving the crowded restaurant, Charlie suggested that she leave her car in the parking lot and, since his closing was nearby, he would drive her back after they had seen the house. "No, thanks," Kathy said. "I've got my camera and a bunch of other stuff in the car. I wouldn't feel good leaving it here."

After a twenty-minute drive, Charlie led her onto a street of federal-style rowhouses that showed no signs of the gentrification that was happening in other sections of the Fan. Before she got out of her car, Kathy checked that the clip in her gun was full, then returned it to the holster in the small of her back. As she joined Charlie in front of the house, she felt a slight chill of unease when he said, "I hope you won't be frightened by what I'm going to show you."

"No. No, I'll be fine. From all my reading I pretty much know what to expect. I hope you don't mind if I take some shots outside as well as inside."

He didn't mind.

There was a musty smell as Charlie opened the front door and ushered her into the front room. It wasn't just musty; there was the unmistakable scent of something rotting. A couple of plastic chairs and a card table had been set up in the living room, along with an old battered TV set that had a bent coat hanger for an aerial. The kitchen was decorated with pennies that had been glued halfway up the wall. Cereal spilled out of boxes onto the counter. A carton of milk stood open, flies buzzing around the top. The kitchen linoleum was filthy and worn through in several places. Dishes stacked in the sink were moldy from the drip of a leaky faucet.

"As you can see, the house is going to take a bit of work before it's in shape to put on the market. Let me show you the dungeon."

Charlie opened a door in the hallway, revealing a surprisingly large closet. He switched on a light, stepped inside, reached in his pocket, and pulled out a pocket knife. Kathy saw a ladder leaning against one side of the closet. As she watched Charlie stoop down and use the knife's blade to pry up a 4x4-inch section of the floor near the left side of the closet, her hand clasped the butt of her gun. She watched him pull out the wooden section and set it aside. Then he reached down, grasped a metal ring, twisted it, and started slowly lifting up a trap door that had been concealed ingeniously in the floor of the closet. Again, she heard moans, but supposed they came from Charlie as he heaved up the door.

As Kathy stepped back into the hallway to give him room to lift the door, she glanced into an adjacent bedroom. She was surprised to see a computer. Covering the far wall stood shelves filled with glass tanks that seemed to have something alive in them—something that looked like large mice or rats. Kathy craned her head around the doorjamb and saw more glass tanks against another wall. These were filled with varying sizes of snakes.

"Well, here we are," said Charlie. "Now you can see where the Slavemaster kept his victims."

"Why are snakes being kept in this room?" she asked.

"Snakes? They were here when I bought the place. Rats and mice, too. I guess they were kept here to feed the snakes. I've tried to find homes for all of them, but, so far, I haven't found any takers. Some of these snakes look like they're quite expensive. I'd hate to let them die. Check out the dungeon, and then I'll show them to you."

He stepped aside so that she could look.

Kathy eased the gun out of the holster. A fetid smell rose from the pit—something like sewer gas. A dim light burning in the hole below illumined exactly what he had described in the chatroom a couple of nights before: a concrete pit, about six feet wide and seven feet deep. But what shocked Kathy and made her gasp was that a man was lying in the pit shackled to the wall. She turned quickly, getting the gun in front of her, only to see Charlie's fist heading for her nose. First, pain—then falling; after that, nothing—just blackness.

When she came to, she was lying in the bottom of the dungeon. The trap door had been closed, but the small light still burned overhead. Her gun was gone. So was her purse. Her head throbbed from the fall, and her joints were stiff from lying in a cramped position. Her first thought was, *How do I get out of here?* As she started to stand up, she realized she was shackled to the wall.

"Welcome to the club."

"How'd you get here?"

"Our friend upstairs."

"Charlie Spenser?"

"Charlie Spenser? What do you mean? I'm Charlie Spenser. You Kathy?"

"Yes. You're really Charlie?"

"Our friend upstairs owned this place before the bank took it back. The name on the mortgage is Henry Conroy. I guess he's the Slavemaster. He's irritated, to say the least, that I bought the place. Evidently wants to pay me back. He hacked into my computer. Read all the stuff from our chatroom meeting. Then this morning, when I came over here to try to tidy up the place for you, he was waiting for me. Threw me in here."

"How long have I been here?

"About an hour."

"Anybody know you're here?"

"No. You?"

"No. Anybody know you bought this place?"

"No. No one, outside of a few people at the mortgage company."

Just then they heard the latch turn in the trap door. When they looked up, they saw Henry smiling down at them.

"Hi, gorgeous. Sorry to take so long, but I had to find a place to put your car and get rid of your camera. Have to be extra careful now that I know you're a cop. Nice gun. That wasn't a very nice trick to play on me. But it'll make what happens next all the sweeter."

Henry leaned forward and tossed a rat down into the pit. Kathy screamed involuntarily and shrank back from the scurrying rat.

"You don't like my little friend? Oh, how sad. The poor thing'll be so lonely. Oh, I know! Wait a minute, I'll get him some playmates."

The trapdoor slammed shut. A moment later, it opened again, and Henry stood over them, holding a sack. He lifted the bottom of the sack and shook it. Three snakes fell into the pit.

As the snakes hit the concrete floor of the dungeon, Charlie Spenser screamed, "No! No! Not snakes! Please get them out of here! I'll do anything you say!"

The snakes coiled as Charlie started kicking at them. Kathy yelled, "Charlie, be still! Don't agitate them! Let them go for the rat!"

Charlie kicked the cover off the drain hole in the center of the dungeon, causing the snakes to pull back to the far wall of the dungeon and coil again.

Above them, Henry was laughing.

"Like my pets? There're all prime specimens. An eastern diamondback rattler, a cottonmouth water moccasin, and a coral snake. Three real killers. Aren't they lovely?"

Just then, Kathy heard the doorbell. Henry slammed the trap door shut and closed the closet door. Charlie pressed himself against the concrete wall. The rat, in its attempt to get away from the snakes, scurried over and crawled up the inside of Charlie's right trouser leg. Charlie began kicking and screaming all over again. The snakes, threatened, struck at once. The rat flew out from the cuff of trousers and fell in the drain hole. As Charlie continued to kick and scream, the rattler and the coral snake fell from his legs. He stomped them, breaking their backs, but the water moccasin clung to him.

After a while, Charlie stopped kicking and slid down the wall, slumping onto the floor, moaning and crying. Kathy had never felt so helpless in her life. She tried to make herself as small and inconspicuous as possible.

"Charlie, just lie still," she whispered. "The less you move, the longer it takes the venom to do its damage."

Charlie stared ahead dully. "It doesn't matter now. I'm dead. It doesn't matter what I do."

The rattler, enraged from its back being broken, struck repeatedly at Charlie's legs and arms. The water moccasin, which had slithered over into one corner of the dungeon, didn't take long to discover the rat, which had come back into the cell from the drain. The snake struck quickly and soon had the rat's head in its mouth. It unhinged its jaw and began swallowing the rat. Kathy watched as Charlie sank deeper and deeper into a fatal torpor. Soon his eyes closed and his breathing became shallow.

The water moccasin, having eaten the rat, now began to look for a warm place to curl up and digest its meal. It glided up onto Kathy's stomach, where it coiled contentedly underneath her jacket near her chin. Even though every nerve in her body was screaming with fear, she willed herself not to move.

After what seemed like hours, Kathy saw the trapdoor open again.

"Who killed my snakes?"

Kathy barely managed a whisper. "Charlie."

"Where's the water moccasin?"

Kathy saw the open drain and got an idea.

"The rat tried to get away down the drain. The water moccasin followed it down."

"Charlie-boy dead yet?"

"I don't know."

Kathy watched as Henry edged the ladder down into the pit. He climbed down it and put his thumb against Charlie's neck to feel his pulse.

"Yup. Dead. Dead. Dead. Serves him right."

Henry turned to Kathy.

"Now it's just you and me, gorgeous."

He reached out put his hand around her neck. Kathy jerked violently away from him. He grabbed her neck with his other hand and moved his face toward her. Just as he was about to kiss her, he let out a loud scream. The water moccasin, roused from its rest, struck Henry just below his right jaw. Henry jerked back, grabbed the snake, and pulled it away. The snake, twisting this way and that, struck again, hitting Henry in a vein under his arm.

Yowling with pain and frustration—the snake still hanging onto him—Henry scrambled up the ladder and through the trapdoor. Kathy could hear him running and screaming for help.

Just as Henry burst out of the front door, Kathy's partner was walking up the sidewalk again. He had been the one who had rung the doorbell earlier. Henry ran down the front steps and out into the street where he collapsed. After alerting the rescue squad and the Richmond police, Kathy's partner went in the house to investigate.

As Kathy was being helped to a waiting ambulance, she saw the dead body of the water moccasin. It had been pulled off Henry Conroy and killed. She bent down and ran her fingers along its smooth iridescent skin and spoke a silent *thank you* to the creature that had saved her life.

Flash Bulletin!

Most of you have read the scare mail about the person whose kidneys were stolen while he was passed out. While that was an "urban legend," this one is not. It's happening every day. I'm sending this "warning" only to a few of my closest friends. You too may have been a victim—read on.

My thighs were stolen from me during the night of August 3rd a few years ago. It was just that quick. I went to sleep in my body and woke up with someone else's thighs. The new ones had the texture of cooked oatmeal. Who would have done such a cruel thing to legs that had been wholly, if imperfectly, mine for years? Whose thighs were these? What happened to mine?

I spent the entire summer looking for them. I searched, in vain, at pools and beaches, anywhere I might find female limbs exposed. I became obsessed. I had nightmares filled with cellulite and flesh that turns to bumps in the night. Finally, hurt and angry, I resigned myself to living out my life in jeans and Sheer Energy pantyhose.

Then, just when my guard was down, the thieves struck again. My rear end was next. I knew it was the same gang, because they took pains to match my new rear end (although badly attached at least three inches lower than the original) to the thighs they had stuck me with earlier. Now my rear end complemented my legs, lump for lump. Frantic, I prayed that long skirts would stay in fashion.

Two years ago I realized my arms had been switched. One morning while fixing my hair, I watched, horrified but fascinated, as the flesh of my upper arms swung to and fro with the motion of the hairbrush. This was really getting scary. My body was being replaced, cleverly and fiendishly, one section at a time. In the end, in deepening despair, I gave up my T-shirts. What could they do to me next? Age? Age had nothing to do with it. Age is supposed to creep up, unnoticed and intangible, something like maturity. NO, I was being attacked, repeatedly, and WITHOUT WARNING.

That's why I've decided to share my story; I can't take on the medical profession by myself. Women of the world, wake up and smell the coffee!! That isn't really plastic those surgeons are using. You know where they're getting those replacement parts, don't you? The next time you suspect someone has had a face "lifted," look again!!! Was it lifted from you? Check out those tummy tucks and buttocks raisings. Look familiar? Are those your eyelids on some movie star? I think I may have finally found my thighs—and I hope that Cindy Crawford paid a really good price for them!!

THIS IS NOT A HOAX!!!! This is happening to women in every town every night.

Pass This Along to Your Women Friends

Yesterday afternoon, around 3:30 P.M. in the Wal-mart parking lot at Forest Drive, I was approached by two males who asked me what kind of perfume I was wearing. When I told them, they inquired if I'd like to sample a fabulous new scent. I probably would have, had I not received an e-mail some weeks ago warning of a "smell-this-neat-perfume" scam. As I walked away, the two men continued to stand between parked cars (probably waiting for someone else to hit on). I stopped a lady going towards them, pointed at them, and told her about how I was sent an e-mail at work about someone walking up to you at the malls or in parking lots, and asking you to sniff perfume that they are selling at a cheap price.

THIS IS NOT PERFUME—IT IS ETHER!

When you sniff it, you pass out. Then they'll take your wallet, your valuables, and heaven knows what else. If it were not for this e-mail, I would probably have sniffed the perfume. But thanks to the generosity of an e-mailing friend, I was spared whatever might have happened to me. I want to do the same for you.

PASS THIS ALONG TO ALL YOUR WOMEN FRIENDS, AND PLEASE STAY ALERT!

Yes, We Have Bad Bananas

WARNING!

Shipments of bananas from Costa Rica have been infected with necrotizing fasciitis, otherwise known as flesh-eating bacteria. This disease recently decimated Costa Rica's monkey population. Scientists have found that the disease grafts itself to the skin of fruits in the region, most notably the banana, Costa Rica's largest export. Until this finding, doctors were not sure how the infection was transmitted. Do not purchase bananas for the next three weeks. This is the period of time for which bananas shipped to the U.S. carry this disease.

If you have eaten a banana in the past three or four days and come down with a fever followed by a skin infection seek medical attention!!! The skin infection from necrotizing fasciitis is very painful and eats two to three inches of flesh per hour. Amputation is likely, death is possible. If you are more than an hour from a medical center, it is advised that you burn the flesh ahead of the infected area to help slow the spread of the infection. The FDA has been reluctant to issue a warning due to fear of a nationwide panic; but they have admitted secretly that around 15,000 Americans will be affected by this disease but that these are "acceptable numbers."

Please forward this warning to people you care about if you feel as we do that 15,000 people is not an acceptable number.

Please Be Super Careful!

Don't go to the bathroom on October 28th. CIA intelligence reports that a major plot is planned for that day. Anyone who takes a poop on the 28th will be bitten on the rear end by an alligator. Reports indicate that organized groups of alligators are planning to rise up into unsuspecting Americans' toilet bowls and bite people as they are doing their business.

I usually don't send e-mails like this, but I got this information from a reliable source. It came from a friend of a friend whose cousin is dating this girl whose brother knows this guy whose wife does the hair of this lady whose husband buys hotdogs from this guy who knows a shoeshine guy who shines the shoes of a mailroom worker who has a friend whose drug dealer sells drugs to another mailroom worker who works in the CIA building. He apparently overheard two guys talking in the bathroom about alligators and came to the conclusion that we are going to be attacked.

So it must be true.

Amish Virus

You have just received the Amish Virus.

Because we Amish don't have any computers, or any programming experience, this virus works on the honor system. Please delete all the files from your hard drive and manually forward this virus to everyone on your mailing list.

Thank you for your kind cooperation.

112